Ghost Stories & Graveyard Tales: New York City

Allen Sircy

Table of Contents

Introduction

Known by many names — The Big Apple, New
Amsterdam, Gotham, The City That Never Sleeps — New
York City is more than just a bustling metropolis.
Beneath its towering skyscrapers and busy streets lies a
hidden world of haunted history, filled with tales of
restless spirits, macabre legends, and the chilling echoes
of long-forgotten crimes.

As we journey through the dark alleys and shadowed
corners of this iconic city, we will uncover stories that
have been buried for centuries, forgotten in the annals of
time. From old cemeteries where body snatchers once
plied their grisly trade to the notorious Manhattan Well
Murder, spectral figures, wronged in life and death, are
said to haunt the site.

New York also has its own tales of macabre
experimentation reminiscent of Mary Shelley's
Frankenstein. At the turn of the 20th doctors conducted
experiments on recently deceased inmates, attempting to
revive them with electricity. These grim endeavors were
more than mere medical trials; they were harbingers of
horror, leaving behind an aura of unease and the
whispers of those who were brought back only to slip
away once more.

The waters of the Long Island Sound hold their own
mysteries. Tales of a menacing sea monster have
persisted for generations, with sightings reported as early
as the 19th century. Descriptions of this creature vary,

from a serpentine behemoth to a leviathan-like being, but all accounts agree on its terrifying presence.

As we navigate through the haunted history of New York City, from its graveyards to its waters, from its hospitals to its prisons, we will uncover the chilling stories that lie just beneath the surface of this iconic city. Join us as we delve into the shadows of the Big Apple, where the past is never truly dead.

Here it is, Ghost Stories & Graveyard Tales: New York City! I hope you have as much fun reading it as I did writing it.

Graveyard Tales

Washington Square Park

Located in the heart of New York City's Greenwich Village, you will find Washington Square Park. The park is renowned for its iconic arch, bustling fountain, and eclectic mix of musicians, artists, and performers. Yet beneath its lively surface lies a rich and eerie history, filled with tales of tragedy, hauntings, and macabre events that have left an indelible mark on this beloved place.

In the late 18th century, what is now Washington Square Park was far from the vibrant community gathering place it is today. In 1797, the city designated the area as a Potter's Field, a burial ground for the poor, the unidentified, and victims of yellow fever epidemics. Thousands of bodies were interred here, their final resting places marked with simple, unadorned graves.

Over the years, numerous construction projects in and around Washington Square Park have unearthed macabre reminders of its past. In 2008, workers testing the soil on the eastern edge of the park uncovered a grim discovery: graves containing the skeletons of 16 individuals. The bones, dating back to the early 19th century, were a stark reminder of the park's origins as a burial ground.

In 2015, more bones were discovered while workers repaired a water main. This time, the skeletal remains of 20 individuals were found in wooden coffins in a stone burial vault. Ten more skeletons were also found near the edge of the park.

One of the park's most infamous landmarks is the Hangman's Elm, an ancient English elm tree standing in the northwest corner. Legend has it that this tree, one of the oldest living trees in Manhattan, served as gallows during the early 19th century. Public executions were reportedly carried out here, with the  condemned meeting their end beneath the tree's sprawling branches. The elm's gnarled limbs and twisted trunk seem to whisper secrets of the past, and some say that on quiet nights, you can still hear the creaking of ropes and the faint cries of the executed.

According to New York lore, the park is said to be a hub of paranormal activity, especially when the city is working on the park and accidentally disturbs any of the remains buried there. From apparitions to phantom footsteps and ghostly whispers when no one is around, Washington Square Park is a must-visit for any paranormal enthusiast.

The Lakeview Cemetery Phantom

In February 1895 residents of Lakeview Heights began to whisper among themselves about a peculiar sight - a figure cloaked in white, haunting the cemetery under the cloak of darkness.

The tale of the phantom spread like wildfire through the town, each retelling more embellished than the last. As fear gripped the hearts of the townsfolk, they flocked to the cemetery each night, hoping to catch a glimpse of the ghost.

On March 2nd a somber funeral service was held for four sailors who had frozen to death after a tragic shipwreck. Among the mourners was Clarence Gerard, a friend of one of the fallen sailors.

After the service, Clarence and two of his friends lingered, hoping to see the ghost that had the area buzzing. It was then that they spotted a peculiar movement by a nearby stream - a white figure gliding silently through the night.

Determined to unravel the mystery, Clarence and his friends gave chase. As they pursued the ghostly figure, it darted upstream, leading them away from the confines of the cemetery.

With each step, Clarence's suspicions grew. Was this truly a restless spirit, or someone playing a joke? Undeterred, he pressed on, his resolve unyielding in the face of fear as his friends fled in fear.

As they neared the cemetery once more, the ghost abruptly changed course, weaving in and out of the tombstones. With a burst of adrenaline, Clarence pursued the phantom onto Waverly Avenue, where it shed its spectral guise and vanished into the night.
Breathless and exhilarated, Clarence found a discarded sheet lying on the ground.

The revelation sent shockwaves through Lakeview Heights, dispelling the specter of fear that had gripped everyone. Yet, even as the mystery of the phantom was laid to rest, questions lingered. Who was under the sheet?

In the end, the identity of the prankster behind the ghostly charade remained shrouded in mystery. However, local authorities believed the "ghost" was really an African American man with mental problems who had been arrested before for chasing women and children in the area.

Ransomed Remains

In the mid-19th century, Alexander Turney Stewart stood out as a pioneering merchant in New York City, creating a retail empire that revolutionized the shopping experience. Stewart's innovative approach to business included

set pricing which eliminated haggling. This truly set him apart from his competitors. He also had a knack for endearing himself to his customers by giving free items like buttons and fabric once the sale was made. Stewart's business acumen was so respected that President Ulysses S. Grant sought him for the position of Secretary of the Treasury when he was elected President. However, a little-known provision dating back to George Washington's presidency prevented his confirmation due to his history of importing goods from other countries. Undeterred, Stewart continued to amass wealth, investing in real estate, hotels, and developing his own community called "Garden City" on Long Island.

In March 1876, Stewart's health began to decline after catching a cold that morphed into a bladder infection. As rumors about his condition swirled, his team planted stories in the press, claiming he was recovering. Sadly, on April 10, Stewart passed died at his 5th Avenue mansion at the age of 72. His funeral was a grand affair, with

nearly 3,000 people walking the streets of New York to St. Mark's Churchyard, where over 15,000 mourners, including notable figures like Hamilton Fish, President Grant's Secretary of State and John Dix, the former governor of New York, paid their respects.

Despite having no children, after Stewart's death numerous alleged relatives came out of the woodwork, attempting to secure part of his $50 million estate. Judge Henry Hilton, a close friend and business partner, ensured these lawsuits did not succeed and that Stewart's widow, Cornelia retained the majority of the estate.

In 1877, Cornelia Stewart began construction on an elaborate crypt at the Cathedral of the Incarnation in Garden City to honor her late husband. This polygon-shaped structure, featuring sixteen sides was supported by high-quality marble pillars, embodying both opulence and eternal permanence. The interior, with its soaring 20-foot ceiling, housed stone shelves designed to hold the remains of her and her husband. However, delays pushed the completion to 1878.

During the summer of that year, George W. Hammill, the sexton of St. Mark's Churchyard received an anonymous letter warning of a plot to steal Stewart's remains. Hammill and his assistant, Francis Parker kept a vigilant watch, but nothing out of the ordinary happened until the morning of October 7, 1878, when the tranquility of the churchyard was shattered by a disturbing discovery. Hammill noticed that the earth around the Stewart family vault had been disturbed, and it appeared that someone had attempted to pry it open. Although the vault itself had not been breached, this unsettling attempt echoed the anonymous warning he had received about a plot to steal Alexander T. Stewart's remains.

Acting swiftly, Hammill consulted with Judge Henry Hilton, the executor of Stewart's estate. They devised a plan to outwit any potential grave robbers. Hammill moved the lavish slab covering the vault to a different location within the graveyard, marking the Stewart family vault with a plain, inconspicuous slab reading "No. 112 Alexander T. Stewart's Family Vault." Additionally, a night watchman was hired to guard the site for a month. Despite these precautions, nothing further seemed amiss, and the watchman was dismissed. However, just a week after the watchman was let go, during a violent storm on the night of November 6, 1878, the daring grave robbers executed their plan.

The next morning, around 7 o'clock, Francis Parker, the assistant sexton was conducting his routine walk through the cemetery when he noticed something terribly wrong. The earth near the Stewart family vault appeared disturbed, and there were clear signs that someone had tampered with the grave. With a sinking feeling, Parker rushed to the site, where he saw that the covering slab of the vault had been removed.

Realizing the gravity of the situation, Parker immediately locked the cemetery gates to prevent any further intrusion and ran to the home of his boss, George

Hammill. Together, they hurried to the residence of Judge Henry Hilton on 34th Street to inform him of the grave robbery. Hilton, both a family friend and the executor of Alexander T. Stewart's estate, understood the seriousness of the situation and accompanied them back to the cemetery to investigate.

Upon their return, Hilton and Hammill opened the vault and descended into its depths. The scene that met them was grim: Stewart's lavish coffin was missing and the vault that held the remains of Stewart family members was in disarray. After ascending the stairs back into the churchyard, they discovered Stewart's red cedar coffin, once adorned with gold fringe, bullion, and gold-plated handles, discarded against a wall near the cemetery steps. The coffin had been pried open, its lead lining cut, and Stewart's remains removed.

The authorities quickly arrived and began their investigation. Inspectors noted the eerie scene: despite the heavy rainstorm the night before, which had left the ground soft and muddy, no footprints were visible leading away from the graveyard. The locked gates added to the mystery, suggesting that the grave robbers had somehow managed to bypass these obstacles without leaving a trace. The only clues left behind were a shovel, a lantern, an old newspaper, and a lone stocking.

The condition of the vault indicated that Stewart's body was in an advanced state of decomposition, and the air was thick with the smell of rotting flesh. A valuable silver nameplate, which had been placed on the coffin, was also missing. The police quickly deduced that the body was not stolen for dissection by medical students, who typically sought fresher corpses. Instead, they speculated that the body had been taken for ransom, given the wealth of Stewart's widow and the prominence of his estate.

Despite the intensity of the storm and the presence of gas lamps along the entire block between Tenth and Eleventh Streets, no one had witnessed the grave robbers. The body snatchers had used the cover of the storm to carry out their plan undetected. The cemetery, with its eight-foot-high iron fence topped with six-inch spikes, seemed an unlikely target, but the robbers had succeeded in their brazen act.

That morning, Judge Hilton took immediate steps to manage the situation. He met with the inspectors and a handful of detectives were assigned to the case. Sexton Hammill and his assistant were interrogated but were quickly cleared of any suspicion. The news of the robbery spread rapidly, and soon, the churchyard was swarming with curiosity seekers and reporters, all eager for details about the high-profile crime. Opportunistic salesmen took advantage of the situation and began placing flyers and pamphlets advertising their wares in the churchyard fence.

Around noon, Judge Hilton went to the Stewart mansion and told Alexander's 75-year-old widow the horrible news personally. Deeply shaken, she demanded that a large reward be issued for the recovery of her husband's remains.

Determined to recover his friend's remains, Hilton offered a substantial reward of $25,000 for information leading to the recovery of Stewart's body and the prosecution of the culprits, emphasizing that no part of the reward would be paid to grave robbing blackmailers.

Soon, authorities were inundated with letters and tips from all over. Thomas Crosby of Elizabeth, New Jersey, wrote a letter to the editor of the New York Herald, claiming that a man named Phillip Schwable could reveal the location of Stewart's remains for $5,000. Detectives investigated Schwable, but the lead proved unfruitful.

Another letter arrived from Stan Colony in Boston, claiming he had crucial information about the body-snatching case and was willing to disclose what he knew for $1,000. This lead, like many others, failed to produce any concrete results.

Inspector Duke of the NYPD received a particularly ominous letter, written and addressed in cutout newsprint characters, claiming, "In eight hours I will be in Canada with AT Stewart's body." Despite the dramatic nature of the note, the tip did not lead to any substantial findings.

One letter published in the New York Herald suggested that Stewart's body would be returned if Mrs. Stewart donated $500,000 to a specified charity. This demand was never acted upon as the family and authorities were wary of paying any ransom.

Several spiritualists emerged, claiming to have channeled Alexander T. Stewart himself. They offered messages purportedly from the deceased, providing various, often contradictory, pieces of information about the body's whereabouts. These claims were generally dismissed as attempts to capitalize on the situation.

A particularly strange tip came in the form of a package containing what was claimed to be pieces of Stewart's coat, pants, vest, shirt, and necktie. This package was accompanied by a letter offering more information in exchange for money, but the authenticity of the clothing pieces was highly suspect.

On November 18, Patrick O'Neil, whose brother was an undertaker, visited the 18th Precinct Police Station. He told the sergeant that he knew of two men involved in the Stewart body snatching case: Thomas Davies and George DeGroff, both undertaker assistants. Detectives quickly investigated but found both men had solid alibis and were well-respected in their community. DeGroff, who was crippled, physically could not have participated in the grave robbery.

Shortly after O'Neil's trip, Henry Vreeland, a 25-year-old cooper, and William Burke, a 40-year-old speculator, were arrested and confessed to the crime. They initially offered to take detectives to the body's hiding place in Chatham, New Jersey. However, once they realized they faced jail time rather than a reward, they retracted their statements and refused to cooperate. No evidence linked them to the crime, leading to their release.

In January 1879, a significant development occurred when Paul Henry Jones, the Postmaster of New York, received a letter from Montreal. The sender, claiming to be in possession of Stewart's body, asked Jones to serve as his attorney and negotiator. Jones responded, requesting proof of the claim. In response, the sender enclosed Stewart's missing nameplate from the coffin. Despite this compelling evidence, Hilton accused Jones of conspiracy and refused to pay any ransom, causing negotiations to falter and the trail to grow cold.

During the investigation, suspicion fell on a man known as "Dr. Douglas," believed to be George A. Christian, a notorious body snatcher from Washington D.C. Douglas had taken up residence in a boarding house across from St. Mark's and advertised for new patients. Suspicion grew when boarders noted that he held secretive meetings with four known criminals. However, by the time the police investigated, Douglas had fled to Pittsburgh, leaving no further clues.

Further efforts to recover the remains continued. In 1884, Judge Hilton negotiated with Lewis C. Swegles, a known grave robber imprisoned in Illinois. Swegles claimed to know where Stewart's body was and was willing to talk in exchange for a pardon and part of the reward. However, the negotiations faltered as the family of an alleged accomplice who had moved Stewart's body became fearful of being arrested.

Former NYPD Police Chief Walling later recounted that Cornelia Stewart personally negotiated for her husband's remains in 1884. According to Walling, a map led her nephew to a clandestine meeting where masked men handed over a bag of bones, which were quietly reinterred in the Cathedral of the Incarnation in 1885. However, this account remains disputed. Henry Hilton's personal assistant, Herbert Antsey, insisted that A. T. Stewart never would have paid the ransom and that he believed that the body was never recovered.

When Cornelia Stewart died in 1886, she was laid to rest beside her husband's supposed grave inside the Cathedral of the Incarnation, although the exact location remains a secret. According to legend, the Stewarts lie beneath the altar of the Cathedral, with a mechanism in place that will ring the church bells if another robbery attempt occurs.

Forgotten Phantoms

Ghosts of the Brooklyn Theatre

In the late 1860s a group of wealthy investors saw an opportunity to transform the St. John's Church and adjoining burying ground into a theatre. With visions of profit dancing in their heads, they acquired the land and made plans to erect the grand Brooklyn Theatre upon the old graveyard.

Despite ample time given for families to relocate the remains of their loved ones, many bodies remained undisturbed beneath the earth as the theatre rose above them.

Although ownership gave little thought to building their new venue over an old burial ground, Sara Conway, wife of Frederick B. Conway, the manager of the new theatre, was hesitant. Sara believed the ground to be cursed, and she vehemently opposed the desecration of the burial site. Unfortunately, her protests fell on deaf ears.

When the theatre was finished, the Conways made their home a second-floor apartment. Yet, tragedy seemed to follow them. Two years after the theatre's grand opening, Frederick Conway fell while walking on stage and became bedridden as his health quickly deteriorated.

Before his death, Frederick confessed his belief that he might have lived a much longer life had he not disregarded the warnings of his wife and the whispers of forgotten graves beneath their feet. His passing left Sara and their children in dire financial straits, forcing them to carry on in the theatre in the face of mounting debts and despair.

Two years later, Sara joined her husband in death. As she lay dying, she spent her final moments lamenting to her children the decision to build the theatre over St. John's graveyard. Eerily, as Sara drew her last breath, the theatre echoed with unearthly moans and shrieks, sending the staff fleeing out of the building.

In the wake of Sara's passing, Edward Thorpe took up the mantle of theatre manager. Unaware of what awaited him, the staff warned him of a shadowy figure haunting the theatre's halls. Edward soon found himself confronted by the ghostly shadow of a woman, her form drifting through the darkness.

But Sara's spirit wouldn't be the only one on the site.

"THE TWO ORPHANS."

There would soon be many more.

On December 5, 1876, the Brooklyn Theatre was packed with over one thousand theatregoers eager to witness a performance of the popular play "The Two Orphans." The play, a melodrama written by Adolphe d'Ennery and Eugène Cormon, was a favorite among audiences of the time. Its tale of two sisters navigating the trials and tribulations of life amid the backdrop of the 18th century. Little did the attendees know that the events unfolding before them would soon turn from theatrical drama to real-life horror.

As the performance reached its climax, a kerosene gaslight ignited a piece of scenery. Strangely, even though the actors were aware of the fire, they continued to perform. Staying in character, Kate Claxton, who portrayed Louise, a blind orphan, told the audience, "The fire is steadily gaining." The actors played the fire off as part of the performance as stagehands struggled to gain control of the blaze. Moments later, smoldering debris began to fall onto the stage. Realizing something was amiss, many seated in the parquette rose from their seats and began to leave. As others began to realize the building was on fire, the theatre was engulfed in flames, and thick smoke billowed throughout the building. The fire spread quickly, fueled by the flammable materials used in building the theatre.

In the frenzy to escape, panic gripped the audience. The exits, which were insufficient for the number of people present, quickly became bottlenecks as patrons fought desperately to flee the inferno. Many were trampled in the stampede, while others were overcome by smoke inhalation or consumed by the flames.

The situation was made even more dire by the lack of fire safety measures in place at the time. The theatre lacked adequate fire escapes, and the narrow stairways leading to the exits became impassable as the fire raged on. As the flames engulfed the building, those trapped inside faced a harrowing choice between being burned alive or leaping to almost certain death from the upper floors.

Chaos reigned supreme as emergency responders and concerned citizens rushed to the scene to assess the damage and search for survivors.

The once bustling theatre now lay in ruins, its grand facade reduced to a pile of broken bricks and splintered wood. Dust and debris filled the air, obscuring the sight of those who bravely ventured into the wreckage in search of signs of life.

Amidst the rubble, a team of dedicated professionals meticulously documented each recovery, carefully preserving any identifying information that could offer solace to grieving families. Personal belongings, fragments of clothing, and even the faintest traces of jewelry were tenderly collected, each item a silent testimony to a life lost too soon.

As rescue teams sifted through the rubble in search of survivors, they stumbled upon fragments of weathered stone hidden beneath the layers of dust and debris. At first glance, they appeared to be nothing more than ordinary rocks, but upon closer inspection, their true nature was revealed.

Etched into the surface of these weathered stones were the names and dates of those laid to rest in the long-forgotten St. John's Burying Ground.

As the recovery efforts continued, families anxiously awaited news of their loved ones, their hearts heavy with grief and uncertainty.

While there are conflicting reports of how many people died in the fire, it is believed that the range is somewhere from 278 to 293. However, 103 of those remains were unidentified. Those unfortunate souls found their final resting place in a common grave at Green-Wood

Cemetery. At its center stands a majestic granite obelisk, towering as a symbol of remembrance and reverence for the lives lost.

Three years later, Haverly's Theatre rose from the ashes of its predecessor on the site. Right away whispers of a curse began to circulate among superstitious natives. It seemed as though the very ground upon which the theatre stood was cursed, its dark history casting a pall over the performances that graced its stage.

Despite the best efforts of the theatre's management, attendance at Haverly's Theatre dwindled, and popular performances failed to draw the large crowds they once did. Some attributed this decline to the lingering aura of tragedy that surrounded the site, while others whispered of more sinister forces at play.

As night fell, the theatre took on a sinister air, its empty halls echoing with the ghostly whispers of those who had perished in the fire. Employees reported seeing shadows darting around the building, and janitors claimed to witness apparitions walking through the theatre, only to vanish into thin air before their eyes.

One particularly chilling tale spoke of a janitor who, while making his rounds one night, stumbled upon two ghostly figures standing upon the stage, reciting lines from the very play that had been performed on that tragic evening — "The Two Orphans." Frozen in terror, the janitor watched in disbelief as the spectral actors faded into the darkness, leaving behind nothing but an eerie silence.

Outside the theatre, passersby reported strange occurrences, with bright lights flickering in the windows and phantom figures seen sitting in empty seats within. It seemed as though the spirits of the past refused to be silenced, their presence haunting the theatre like a specter from beyond the grave.

Despite attempts to quell the rumors and restore the theatre's reputation, attendance continued to plummet, and it soon became clear that Haverly's Theatre was doomed to the same fate as its predecessor. In 1890, the decision was made to tear down the cursed building and demolish it once and for all, clearing the way for the construction of the Brooklyn Daily Eagle office building. Today, the site of the ill-fated theatre is home to Cadman Plaza.

Tales from the Tombs

Halls of Justice

The New York City Halls of Justice and House of Detention, known to locals as "The Tombs," carries a moniker as enigmatic as its history. The origins of this nickname trace back to its inaugural structure, an Egyptian Revival building designed by architect John Haviland that was completed in 1838. The building's somber, tomb-like appearance quickly earned it its eerie nickname.

The Tombs was built on land formerly occupied by Collect Pond, a vital water source for Colonial New York City which had become severely polluted by the late 18th century due to industrialization and population growth. The pond was condemned, drained, and filled in by 1817, but the landfill job was inadequately executed, leading to subsidence within a decade. The neighborhood,

transformed into the notorious slum of Five Points, suffered from swampy, malodorous conditions that seeped into the prison's foundation. Naturally, with so much moisture, the facility was plagued by unsanitary conditions.

The Tombs encompassed a full city block defined by Centre Street, Franklin Street, Elm Street (now Lafayette Street), and Leonard Street. It measured 253 feet 3 inches in length and 200 feet 5 inches in width, and it initially housed approximately 300 prisoners. Yet, as the city grew so did the number of prisoners. The facility was often overcrowded and at one point the Board of Health got involved, leading officials to come up with a larger prison on the site.

The original facility was replaced by the City Prison in 1902. However, locals clung to the original building's nickname and continued to call it "The Tombs".

In 1941 the prison was replaced by the Manhattan House of Detention, a modern high-rise structure situated across the street on the east side of Centre Street. Eventually remodeled, it served as the Manhattan Detention Complex from 1983 until its closure in 2023. Plans to demolish the complex in April 2023 were stalled due to community concerns, marking yet another chapter in the storied past of this site.

Throughout the years the Tombs have held some very dangerous prisoners, and many men were hanged inside the courtyard of the prison. One of the most famous prisoners scheduled to be hanged on the grounds was the infamous John C. Colt.

In the early 19th century, the name Colt was synonymous with innovation and enterprise. Samuel Colt, a visionary inventor, had already made his mark on history with his revolutionary designs for the Colt revolver. But behind the scenes of his success stood his older brother, John C. Colt, a man whose ambition burned just as fiercely as his brother's, yet whose path would ultimately lead him down a darker road.

John Caldwell Colt was born into the Colt family in 1810. From a young age, John showed a keen intellect and a natural flair for business. While his brother Samuel pursued his passion for invention, John immersed himself in the world of commerce, eager to make his mark on America's burgeoning industrial landscape.

As Samuel's fortunes soared with the success of his firearms business, John sought to carve out his own niche in the business world. He dabbled in various ventures, from importing luxury goods to investing in real estate, each endeavor fueled by his relentless drive to succeed. However, John's ambitions knew no bounds, and he hungered for greater success. Inspired by his brother's achievements, he set his sights on the burgeoning publishing industry, believing that writing textbooks about bookkeeping would bring wealth and influence.

With Samuel's financial backing, John began to write and slowly started to step out of his brother's shadow. But beneath the veneer of success lurked a darker side to John's character. His insatiable thirst for wealth and power drove him to cut corners and bend the rules, often at the expense of others. Rumors swirled of shady dealings and questionable alliances, yet John remained untouchable, shielded by his family's money. It was during this time that John's path crossed with that of Samuel Adams, a local printer who he had been working with to publish his textbooks.

On September 17, 1841, Adams entered Colt's office on the corner of Chambers Street and Broadway to collect a debt owed to him for the books he had printed. Adams demanded payment of $71.15. However, Colt vehemently disagreed, claiming that he only owed Adams $55.85.

As the disagreement escalated into a heated argument, tempers flared, and words turned to blows. According to Colt's later confession, Adams, in a fit of rage, shoved him against the wall and began strangling him.

Feeling overpowered and fearing for his life, Colt reached for a hatchet that lay within reach on his desk. In a moment of desperation, he struck Adams repeatedly  over the head until Adams fell unconscious, blood flowing from gory wounds.

In the aftermath of the violent altercation, Colt was faced with a decision. His first instinct was to notify the authorities of what had transpired, but then he hesitated. The weight of his family's reputation bore down upon him, the fear of tarnishing their name too great to bear. Seeking counsel from his elder brother, Samuel Colt, who was staying at the City Hotel, John Colt went to him for guidance. However, Samuel was busy meeting with prospective investors. With adrenaline still coursing through his veins, John found himself unable to wait for his brother. He hastily left the hotel and went back to his office.

At the scene of the murder, John Colt was consumed by a maelstrom of conflicting emotions - guilt, fear, and a gnawing sense of remorse. With the blood of the printer staining the floorboards beneath him, he grappled with the consequences of his actions, knowing that his life would never be the same again.

Having very few options, Colt cleaned the blood from the floor and walls and then found himself faced with the grim task of disposing of Adams' body. In a desperate attempt to cover up his crime, Colt hatched a macabre plan to ship Adams' body out of New York City.

Drawing upon his knowledge of shipping and logistics, Colt set about arranging for Adams' remains to be transported to a nonexistent address at a remote location in New Orleans, where they would be unlikely to be discovered. Colt enlisted the help of a carman, who unknowingly assisted him in transporting the body in a shipping crate packed with salt to a ship named the *Kalamazoo*.

Using false identities and forged documents, Colt attempted to conceal his involvement in the crime and evade detection by law enforcement.

As the investigation into the disappearance of Samuel Adams unfolded in the following days, his family became increasingly frantic, desperate for any sign of their missing loved one. Flyers were circulated, rewards were offered, and inquiries were made, all in a frantic effort to locate Adams and bring him home.

Meanwhile, suspicions began to swirl around John Colt, whose tumultuous relationship with Adams and suspicious behavior in the aftermath of the murder had not gone unnoticed by those closest to him. Among them was a man named Asa Wheeler, a handwriting teacher who had a room next door to Colt's office. Wheeler heard the men arguing and stationed himself outside Colt's office. Although he didn't witness the murder happen, through a keyhole, Wheeler observed Colt bending over a fallen Samuel Adams acting erratically.

Once Colt left to go see his brother, the nosey neighbor procured a key to the office from the landlord. Upon entering, he noticed that a mirror had been shattered and that the floor had recently been cleaned.

Unsure of what had taken place, Wheeler wasted no time in alerting the authorities, providing crucial evidence that

would ultimately lead to Colt's apprehension and arrest.
Even more damning, the shipping crate that carried
Adams' rotting cadaver was held up on the docks.
Oddly, those on the ship noticed it's horrible stench but
chalked up to poison used to kill rodents.

When authorities arrived at the ship, they opened the
crate and found a decomposing body covered in salt. A
gold ring and scars on the body's leg was used to identify
the remains of Samuel Adams.

Despite his protestations of self-defense, John's past caught up with him, and he found himself standing trial for the murder of Samuel Adams. It was a trial that gripped the nation. The accused: John C. Colt, a member of the renowned Colt family, charged with the brutal murder of Samuel Adams, a printer that wanted to collect on a debt.

The courtroom buzzed with anticipation as the trial commenced, the air thick with tension and speculation. John, his once-handsome features now etched with strain and fatigue, stood before the judge and jury, his fate hanging in the balance.

The prosecution painted a damning picture of John as a desperate man, driven to murder by his creditor. When the prosecutor presented a blood-stained hatchet that was found in Colt's home, it appeared to be an open and shut case. Even more damning was Samuel Adams' watch that was found in Colt's trunk in his residence.

But as the trial wore on, cracks began to appear in the prosecution's case. Defense attorneys painted John as a victim of circumstance, a man who was fighting for his life. They pointed to inconsistencies in the evidence and raised doubts about the credibility of key witnesses, casting doubt upon the prosecution's version of events. The defense insisted Colt was merely defending himself from an aggressive Samuel Adams who was trying to choke their client. They also claimed Colt didn't intend to hit Adams with a hatchet. During their scuffle, he reached for a hammer lying on the desk. However, eager to defend himself, he grabbed the hatchet by mistake and began trying to strike his attacker.

In an odd twist, Samuel Colt was called in to testify and demonstrate his pistol when a hole was discovered in Adams' head. However, after Colt testified, it was determined that the hole was due to a nail in the shipping crate that went through the wood and into his head, not a ball from a pistol.

At the conclusion of the trial, the judge gave the jury clear instructions that Colt should be found guilty of manslaughter since there were no signs that the murder was premeditated. However, he let it be known that murder in the first degree was still a viable verdict. When the jury's unanimous verdict was delivered, he was found guilty of murder. John C. Colt was sentenced to death by hanging. He was promptly led away to the Tombs to await his execution as his attorneys protested and demanded a new trial. While appeals were made to higher courts and the governor, Colt's attorneys were unsuccessful, and it was only a matter of time before he was executed in the courtyard of the Tombs.

As he waited for his day on the gallows, Colt's wealthy family spared no expense in ensuring his comfort behind bars. Reports from the time suggest that he was provided with lavish meals, far beyond the standard fare typically served to prisoners.

But Colt's taste for luxury was matched only by his cunning and ingenuity. Determined to escape the confines of his cell, he devised a daring plan to disguise himself as a woman and sneak past the guards unnoticed. With the help of accomplices on the outside, he acquired women's clothing and accessories, transforming himself into an unassuming lady in an audacious bid for freedom.

However, Colt's carefully laid plans were foiled when his disguise was discovered by the guards, who promptly returned him to his cell. Undeterred, he continued to plot his escape, exploring every possible avenue for freedom, no matter how improbable.

In a shocking twist, rumors began to circulate that Colt had made arrangements with a local doctor to revive him after his scheduled execution by hanging. During that time, scientists and doctors were fascinated with galvanism due to the success of Mary Shelley's "Frankenstein." According to legend, the doctor was to connect a galvanized battery to his temples and spine to resurrect him after he was pronounced dead.

Unable to sleep, Colt spent his last night in the Tombs writing letters and spending time with the keepers. He met with Sheriff Monmouth B. Hart and asked if it would be possible to push his execution back later in the day. Surprisingly, the sheriff agreed.

The morning of November 18, 1842, dawned with an eerie stillness over New York City's infamous Tombs prison, where Colt awaited his final reckoning. However, a joyous occasion was about to unfold, The Colt family arranged for John to get married in the prison before his execution. For months, he had lived with Caroline Henshaw, a Scottish lady who was alleged to be pregnant, and now she would be an honest woman. After the ceremony, the new couple only had a few moments to celebrate before Colt was rushed back to his cell. As the day wore on, Colt met with his brother and new wife before he met with Sheriff Hart. The convicted murderer pleaded with him to postpone the execution to the following day. This time his request was denied.

Dejected, Colt asked the keeper if he could spend some time alone in his cell. Around 3 p.m., Reverend Henry Anthon went to Colt's cell to pray with him. But when he called out to Colt, he didn't answer. When a keeper let him in the cell, Reverend Anthon found Colt unresponsive, laying on his side. When he turned him over, the pastor gasped and stumbled backwards out of the cell. As keepers rushed in to see what was wrong, they found Colt covered in blood. With only an hour left to live, he had committed suicide by stabbing himself in the heart with a knife.

As officials raced to Colt's cell, an alarm was sounded as smoke was detected in the cupola of the prison. The blaze quickly spread and officials on hand for the execution were summoned to help the fire brigade to contain the conflagration. After several hours the flames were finally extinguished.

New York was buzzing. Rumors began to circulate suggesting that the Colt family had someone set the prison on as a diversion so John C. Colt could stage his own death. But officials at the Tombs were adamant that the fire was started due to a stove and a faulty flue.

In the following days it was speculated that Colt killed another inmate and placed him in his cell in the hour before he was discovered by Reverenced Anthon. As officials were trying to sort out the suicide, they abruptly had to fight a fire, allowing Colt to quietly slipped out of the Tombs with the help of prison officials and the pastor who had been paid a handsome sum by the Colt family. Strangely, several firefighters went on record stating that they saw Colt slip out of the prison during the fire and climb into a wagon that sped away.

In the years that followed, sightings of John would emerge sporadically, offering glimpses of a man believed to be long dead. From the bustling streets of New York City to the sun-drenched shores of California, reports of his whereabouts would surface from time to time. Some even claimed that he boarded a ship and went to Europe to live out the rest of his days.

One of the most compelling sightings came from California, where a man bearing a striking resemblance to John C. Colt was allegedly spotted wandering the dusty streets of a remote mining town. Witnesses who had lived in New York claimed that the man had spoken of his past, alluding to a life lived in hiding and on the run from the law.

Despite the fervent speculation and occasional brief sightings, concrete proof of whether John C. Colt was still alive remained elusive. For every sighting, there were skeptics who dismissed it as mere hearsay or wishful thinking.

In an even stranger twist, Caroline Henshaw, John Colt's bride, was believed to be Samuel Colt's mistress. According to legend, Samuel got Caroline pregnant after she came over from Scotland. By marrying John, Caroline's child would carry the Colt name. After John's mysterious death, Caroline and the child, named Samuel Colt moved to Europe. The child was cared for by his "uncle" for years and received a very large inheritance.

Hauntings

In the late 19th century, before the Tombs was torn down and became the City Prison, the building was rife with tales about the supernatural, particularly a courtroom on the second floor.

This particular courtroom was situated directly beneath an old storage room where the gallows were kept. The legend among the prison staff was that this courtroom played host to various unexplained phenomena, especially during the week of executions.

The eerie disturbances were first noted when keepers and court officers reported hearing inexplicable footsteps and strange noises in the courtroom. These sounds were particularly intense around the times when the gallows were in use. One night, following an execution, the gallows had just been returned to their storage when the unsettling sound of disembodied footsteps echoed through the courtroom. Sam Galbraith, a veteran keeper, was called upon to investigate the empty, shadow-laden room.

Armed with only a lantern and a club for protection, Sam entered the courtroom, thinking he might discover a court attendee who had accidentally been locked in after falling asleep. What happened next would become a chilling staple of The Tombs' haunted lore. Moments after Sam entered the room, his colleagues outside heard a blood-curdling scream for help. Rushing to his aid, they found him unconscious on the floor with no one else around.

Sam was quickly attended to by Dr. David Brekes, the prison physician, who noted that Sam appeared to have been violently assaulted; his face was distorted, bruised, and he was in a state of utter terror. When revived, Sam recounted a harrowing encounter with an unseen assailant who had seemingly materialized from the shadows and grabbed him by the throat. Despite an exhaustive search, no evidence of any intruder was found.

The uncanny incidents continued over the years. William Snow, a night keeper, and his team experienced the unexplained rattling and slamming of the courtroom doors, despite thorough checks confirming all potential entrances were secured. Most disturbing, however, was the night following the execution of John Real, a man convicted of killing a patrolman. As the legend goes, the courtroom seemed to stir with a life of its own that evening. When the keepers entered the room to investigate noises they encountered a glowing apparition resembling Real, which vanished before their very eyes.

In a defiant act of skepticism mixed with bravado, Billy Burns, a court reporter, wagered with the warden that he could spend an entire night in the haunted courtroom after an execution. Armed with whiskey, newspapers, candles, and matches to ward off the darkness and perhaps bolster his courage, Billy settled in for the night.

For hours, nothing occurred, until a sudden commotion—a loud crash broke the eerie calm. Keepers

found Billy unconscious, bleeding profusely under a table.

When Billy regained consciousness, he described a chilling sequence of events where his candles were repeatedly extinguished by an unseen force, despite his efforts to relight them.

Aggravated, Billy began to curse at the entity. As he began to raise his voice, an unseen force seized him by the throat and a cold burst of air blew out all the candles.

The tales of the haunted courtroom in The Tombs contributed to its dark mystique, blurring the lines between the harsh realities of prison life and the spectral remnants of its grisly past. Oddly, after the first building was demolished the ghostly activity subsided.

New York Frankenstein

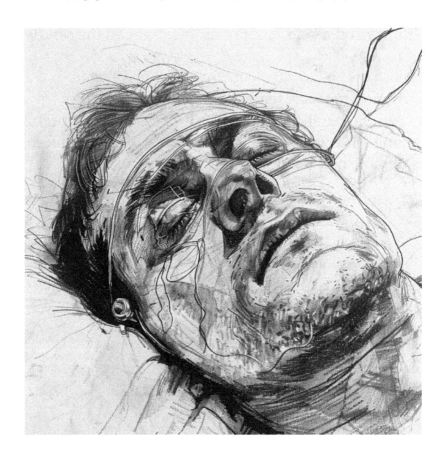

Jolting John Johnson

In the early 19th century, New York City was a bustling port teeming with sailors from around the world. Amidst this vibrant backdrop stood a small boarding house at 65 Front Street, run by John Johnson. Johnson's establishment was a home for wayward sailors, and in 1823, it became the scene of a gruesome crime that would captivate the city.

On November 22, 1823, a sailor named James Murray arrived in New York from Boston. The following day, Murray's lifeless body was discovered in Cuyler's Alley by watchman Charles Miller. The sight was ghastly: Murray's head had been split open with a hatchet, and his body was naked from the waist down. Crimson-soaked flannel drawers and an old pillowcase were tied around his head with a rope. The coroner's examination revealed that Murray had been struck on the left side of his head with a blunt object, fracturing his skull and exposing his brain.

Three witnesses soon came forward, claiming to have seen Murray at the wharf, looking for a ship to New Orleans. Captain Samuel Morehouse and his crew, who had sailed with Murray from Boston, were summoned to identify the body. They confirmed Murray had a large chest and recounted seeing John Johnson, the owner of a boarding house, help him carry it from the wharf.

Local cartman Thomas Kipp also corroborated this, stating he had transported the men and the chest to Johnson's boarding house.

The following day, detectives searched Johnson's boarding house, uncovering bloodstains leading from a second-floor bedroom to the cellar. In the dark cellar, they found a bloody bed sheet wadded in a corner. Outside, hidden in a pile of wood, were Murray's crimson-stained clothes.

Johnson was promptly arrested and initially confessed to the crime. He admitted that Murray had boasted about his money, leading Johnson to steal the key to his chest as his guest slept. When he went downstairs into the front room, he unlocked the chest and discovered two large bags of silver dollars. Johnson then went into his cellar to grab his hatchet.

In the dark of night, he quietly snuck back into his room and struck Murray twice in the head while he slept. When blood began to pour from the wounds, Johnson wrapped his head to contain the bleeding.

However, days later, Johnson retracted his confession. He claimed that he was coerced into it to protect his family from being implicated. He told a local minister that another guest in his boarding house named Jerry had proposed killing Murray and splitting the money. Johnson claimed that Jerry had already killed Murray by the time he returned from checking if any watchmen were patrolling outside. Johnson confessed to helping

Jerry hide the body but insisted he did not deliver the fatal blow.

Johnson's trial drew massive public attention. Thousands gathered outside the courthouse daily, eager for updates on the sensational case. Despite Johnson's pleas of innocence, he was swiftly convicted and sentenced to hang on April 2, 1824.

On the day of his execution, 50,000 spectators—about a third of New York City's population—assembled at an open field near the corner of Second Avenue and 13th Street. Such a massive gathering required an unprecedented level of law enforcement to maintain order. The entire New York City police force was deployed, along with roughly 80 constables, to ensure the execution proceeded without incident.

Johnson was escorted to the gallows by the sheriff, infantrymen, and his minister. His hands and feet were bound, a black bag placed over his head, and a noose secured around his neck. With much of the city watching, he declined to make any final statements. The executioner cut the rope, and Johnson plummeted, his body jerking violently as the rope snapped taut. The silence of the crowd shattered, replaced by a collective gasp. Johnson's body swayed in the air, the noose cutting deeply into his neck. For a few agonizing moments, his legs kicked out in a desperate, futile struggle against death. The spectacle was both horrific and mesmerizing, a macabre dance between life and death.

As life drained from his body, Johnson's movements slowed, then ceased.

After he was pronounced dead, Johnson's body was taken down and handed over to doctors from the medical college. They wasted no time in transporting him to the school. Placed on a cold, wooden table, his body became the subject of a grim experiment. The doctors attached a battery to his spine and temple, sending an electrical current through his lifeless form. To their horror and amazement, Johnson's body responded: his eyelids flickered, his eyes darted, and his mouth moved as if he was trying to talk.

In a final, eerie display, Johnson's hands rose from the table, defying death's dark embrace. The battery's charge soon waned, and his body went limp once more. Johnson's remains were then buried in an unmarked grave in an unknown burying ground.

Revived

Ann Coleman was a 23-year-old Haitian immigrant living in New York City in 1838. Her days were spent selling hot roasted ears of corn on the crowded sidewalks while her husband of five years, Edward, roamed the streets as a notorious gangster. Their relationship was anything but tranquil; it was fraught with turmoil and violence.

Edward Coleman, a few years older than Ann, had crossed paths with her in 1833 when he migrated from Philadelphia to New York. Their residence was on Fulton Street, a place where their arguments frequently escalated into physical altercations. Edward had a reputation for his violent nature, having been incarcerated twice due to his abusive behavior towards Ann.

The climax of their tumultuous relationship unfolded on Sunday, July 16, 1838, when Ann sought refuge at her friend Charlotte Hilton's residence on Howard Street. Terrified for her life after Edward's threatening behavior, Ann begged her friend to help her. After several days of staying there, Ann reluctantly returned home when Edward apologized for his actions.

However, the cycle of violence continued. On July 30th, another heated argument erupted between Ann and Edward. Fearing for her life, Ann fled their home, intending to seek help from the police. As she ran through the streets, screaming for assistance, Edward pursued her relentlessly. Despite her desperate attempts to escape, Edward caught up with her at the corner of Broadway and White Street.

In a shocking display of brutality, Edward grabbed Ann by the hair, exposing her vulnerable neck, as he pulled a straight razor from his pocket. With swift and merciless force, he sliced her throat from ear to ear, leaving her lifeless body sprawled on the dirt street in a pool of blood. Surprisingly, Ann mustered enough strength to stand and take a few steps before her limp, lifeless body collapsed to the ground one last time. Witnesses, including a local grocer, were horrified as they watched Edward callously stand over his wife's corpse.

Authorities quickly apprehended Edward, who made no attempt to resist arrest. Charged with the murder of his wife, Edward pleaded not guilty by reason of insanity. However, prosecutors presented damning evidence, including previous reports of Edward's threats, and eyewitness testimonies of the gruesome murder. Despite attempts by Edward's attorney to portray him in a favorable light, the jury deliberated for a mere ten minutes before convicting him of willful murder.

On January 13, 1839, Edward faced his punishment at the newly constructed Tombs Prison. As he awaited his execution, he clung to the hope of a last-minute pardon, futilely pleading with the sheriff for a delay. When no reprieve arrived, Edward was placed on a horse-drawn wagon and escorted to the hanging tree on the prison grounds.

Clad in a white robe, Edward's hands were bound, and a noose placed around his neck. He was positioned beneath the tree. The sheriff signaled the horse to depart, leaving Edward dangling from the branch, writhing in agony before eventually becoming perfectly still.

Following Edward's execution, the aftermath was a macabre blend of scientific curiosity and societal spectacle. As his lifeless body was removed from the gallows, it was transported back to the confines of the Tombs Prison. However, this was not the end of the story for Edward.

Upon his return, two doctors eagerly awaited the opportunity to conduct galvanic experiments on Edward's corpse.

In a dimly lit room, surrounded by a small gathering of medical students and curious onlookers, the doctors affixed metal rods to Edward's lifeless form. With bated breath, they activated the battery, sending jolts of electricity coursing through his inert body.

The effect was astonishing. Edward's eyes snapped open, his chest heaved as if drawing breath, and his muscles twitched in response to the electrical stimulation.

Spectators watched in awe and horror as the boundaries between life and death seemed to blur before their eyes.

For a fleeting moment, Edward's corpse appeared to exhibit signs of vitality, a ghastly semblance of resurrection. Yet, as the battery's power waned, so did the illusion of life. Edward's body slumped back into stillness, a stark reminder of the irreversible nature of death.

Doctors meticulously examined Edward's remains, confirming his death once more.

The fate of Edward's body is shrouded in mystery. Likely subjected to further dissection and study at a medical school, his mortal remains were likely consigned to an unmarked pauper's grave.

Ghosts of Olde New York

The Dead Dentist

Harvey Burdell was
born in 1811 in
Herkimer County,
New York, into a
modest but respectable
family. In the mid-
1830s, Harvey moved
to New York City and
began practicing
dentistry with his
brother, John, in Lower
Manhattan. The
Burdell brothers'
practice flourished and
after a while, Harvey went out on his own and opened
his own office. In 1852 he bought a four-story brick house
from Timothy Woodruff at 31 Bond Street for $15,500. He
turned the place into a boarding house, taking a room for
himself and another room for his office.

Outside of his professional life, Harvey was known to be
a man of a womanizer and a somewhat flamboyant
personality. He enjoyed the social life that New York City
offered and was often seen around town chasing women.
Despite his success and social standing, Harvey remained
a bachelor, a fact that often made him the subject of
speculation and gossip. It was even rumored that he
treated prostitutes and traded his services for their
company.

In the summer of 1855 Harvey met Emma Cunningham, a 37-year-old widow with four children and they began a whirlwind courtship.

After her husband died in 1852 Emma received a payout of $10,000 from a life insurance policy. But by the time she met Harvey she had burned through most of it and was desperate to find some stability for herself and her children. The affections of a handsome dentist that owned a large house seemed too good to be true.

That fall, Emma found herself pregnant with Harvey's baby and expecting a proposal of marriage. Instead, she faced the heartbreak of an abortion, almost certainly at Burdell's urging and likely performed by the dentist himself. Despite this, Emma remained determined to be with him due to the security he provided for her family.

During this time, Emma leased Burdell's house on Bond Street and moved her children into the home. The household at 31 Bond Street was lively and diverse. It included Emma's four children, Hannah Conlan the cook, and three boarders: George Snodgrass, an 18-year-old poet and banjo player; Daniel Ulman; and John J. Eckel, a tanner who became particularly close to Emma.

Despite leasing the building to Emma, Burdell maintained his own room and dental office on the second floor and continued his practice there. Emma behaved as though she and Burdell were man and wife — ordering food, hiring maids, and dining at his table.

By 1857, the relationship between Emma and Harvey had grown increasingly strained. Emma was intensely jealous of Burdell's 24-year-old cousin, Dimis Hubbard, who frequently visited the house. Emma was also frustrated with Burdell's liaisons with female patients in his office when she was present. Their arguments became a regular occurrence, and Burdell eventually stopped dining with Emma and her children, preferring to eat his meals at a nearby hotel.

On the night of January 30, 1857, around half past ten, a chilling cry of "Murder!" was heard by a man living nearby at 36 Bond Street. The source of the scream was unclear. The next morning, John Burchill, the boy hired to start the fire in Dr. Burdell's office each day, opened the door to a gruesome sight: Harvey's mutilated body lay face down in a pool of blood, with splatters reaching over five feet up the wall. Burchill ran into the dining room and found Emma eating breakfast with George Snodgrass.

The discovery of the body sent shockwaves through the neighborhood as authorities descended upon Bond Street. The examination of Burdell's body determined he had been strangled and stabbed fifteen times with a long, slender knife. Immediately, Emma became the lead suspect. A thorough search of the house and interrogations of all residents followed, led by the coroner's inquest that lasted two weeks. The investigation revealed much about the characters living at 31 Bond Street. Emma produced a marriage certificate, claiming she had secretly married Harvey. A search of George Snodgrass's room uncovered undergarments belonging to Helen Cunningham, Emma's 15-year-old daughter.

Harvey's former business partner, Alvah Blaisdell, told detectives that Burdell confided in him that he was afraid of Emma. Dimis Hubbard testified that Harvey had planned to terminate his agreement with Emma and replace her with another landlady. This was corroborated by a maid who overheard Emma telling Hannah that Harvey may not live long enough to sign the papers. The maids also confirmed that Emma was intimately involved with boarder John Eckel.

The coroner's investigation revealed that the stab wounds on Burdell indicated the assailant was left-handed. Ironically, Emma Cunningham was left-handed. She, along with John Eckel, were charged with murder, while George Snodgrass was charged as an accessory. All three were taken to the Tombs.

Emma was not allowed to attend Dr. Burdell's funeral, which attracted over 8,000 people. However, she was permitted to pay her last respects before the coffin was sealed. In a scene filled with hysteria and tears, she cried out, "Oh I wish to God you could speak, and tell who done it."

The trial that followed captivated the city, drawing widespread media attention and public fascination. The prosecution, led by District Attorney A. Oakey Hall, argued that Emma had a strong motive to kill Burdell. They painted a picture of a woman driven by financial desperation and jealousy. Witnesses testified about the frequent, heated arguments between Emma and Dr. Burdell.

However, the prosecution's case relied heavily on circumstantial evidence. There was no concrete proof directly linking Emma to the murder. The defense, led by the renowned lawyer Henry L. Clinton, seized on this. Clinton portrayed Emma as a respectable widow trying to support her family. He argued that she had no reason to murder Harvey, emphasizing her claim of being his lawful wife, which would have secured her financial stability without resorting to violence. As a widow she was only entitled to a third of his estate.

After weeks of intense legal battles and public scrutiny, the jury deliberated on the evidence presented. The lack of concrete proof and the effective questioning of witness credibility played a crucial role in their decision. Emma Cunningham was ultimately acquitted of the murder charges. The jury found that the prosecution had not provided enough substantial evidence to prove her guilt beyond a reasonable doubt.

The verdict was met with mixed reactions from the public. Some believed in Emma's innocence, while others were convinced she had escaped justice. Despite her acquittal, Emma's life was forever changed. She faced ongoing suspicion and public scrutiny, and the trial left an indelible mark on her reputation.

As for John Eckel and George Snodgrass, they were also acquitted.

While in jail, Emma's belly began to grow and she confided in the jailer that she was carrying Dr. Burdell's child, claiming that the unborn baby would entitle her to inherit his entire estate instead of the smaller share as stated by law. Emma continued this claim even after she was released from custody, knowing that a child would solidify her position as Burdell's widow and heir.

However, she wasn't pregnant. Realizing the need for an accomplice to make her plan work, Emma confided in Dr. David Uhl. She enlisted his help, believing he would procure a baby for her to present as Harvey Burdell's heir when the time came. The doctor, however, had different plans. He went straight to the district attorney and revealed Emma's scheme.

When the time came for Emma to "give birth," The doctor told her he had obtained a baby from a "California Widow". In reality, the district attorney had arranged for a baby from an indigent mother at Bellevue Hospital. Emma, dressed as a Sister of Charity, carried the baby from Dr. Uhl's office in a basket, ready to present it as her own.

The ruse was carried out at 31 Bond Street with Emma faking labor behind a closed door, as she screamed in agony from supposed labor pains. Dr. Uhl emerged with the baby, but the plot quickly fell apart when policemen entered the room and charged Emma with fraud and took her back to the Tombs. The charges were eventually dropped, but the scandal was enough to invalidate her claim of marriage in the eyes of the Surrogate Court, leaving her without any claim to Dr. Burdell's estate.

Following the failed scheme, Emma left New York for California. In 1870, she married again, hoping for a fresh start. However, her second husband died thirteen years later, leaving her widowed once more. Emma Cunningham moved back to New York and died in 1887. She was buried in Green-Wood Cemetery, not far from Dr. Harvey Burdell's grave. The words, "May God Rest Her Troubled Soul," are inscribed in her tombstone.

Hauntings

After Emma Cunningham left New York for California in shame, the infamous house on Bond Street where Dr. Harvey Burdell was murdered became the focus of eerie tales and strange occurrences. Watchmen who patrolled the area after dark reported seeing a shadowy form in the room where Dr. Burdell had met his gruesome end. The house, already a scene of scandal and violence, seemed to take on a life of its own, with whispered rumors of it being haunted circulating among the locals.

Adding to the mystery, a mysterious old woman began to appear in the neighborhood. Every evening, just after dusk, she would shuffle across the street and sit on the doorstep of the house directly opposite 31 Bond Street. Without uttering a word, she sat there with a knife in her hand, methodically cutting up pieces of cooked lamb and eating them one by one. Her eyes never left Dr. Burdell's old house, as if she were waiting or watching for something. When watchmen asked her to move, she would silently scurry over to the neighboring house's porch, always keeping her gaze fixed on Harvey's old boarding house. This bizarre ritual continued for several weeks until the mysterious woman vanished as abruptly as she had appeared.

In 1858, a series of sensational séances in Boston captivated the public's imagination and made headlines worldwide. A group of reputable spiritualists conducted three séances over six weeks, claiming to have summoned the spirit of Harvey Burdell. During these séances, the spirit purportedly revealed chilling details about the day of his murder.

According to the spirit, on the day he was killed, Harvey Burdell had a heated argument with Emma Cunningham, informing her that he planned to evict her and her children from his house. Emma became enraged, shouting at him as he left for the bank, where he withdrew $1,500.

That evening, as Harvey returned home around ten o'clock with the banknotes, he noticed his office boy, John Burchill, following him and then standing outside the house as if keeping watch. Upon entering the house, Burdell passed John Eckel, who looked outside and saw Burchill nod, signaling that no one was observing them.

Once inside his office, Harvey placed the money in his trunk and removed his coat. Suddenly, he was struck from behind on the head with a hammer. As he screamed "Murder!" Emma and her eldest daughter, Augusta, began stabbing him repeatedly with knives. Dr. Burdell's spirit claimed to have watched as he collapsed to the floor, dead. Emma and Augusta then went to the attic to clean up and change their clothes before returning to retrieve the key from his pocket to the trunk. Joined by Eckel and Burchill, they stole not only the $1,500 Burdell had placed there earlier but also another $2,000 and some gold. They took important documents, including his will, and burned them to eliminate any trace of his intention to not marry Emma.

Harvey's spirit insisted that Emma was lying about their marriage, stating unequivocally that he had never married her and that the marriage certificate she presented during the trial was a forgery.

As the séance concluded, Burdell's spirit expressed confusion over why investigators had not discovered the hammer blow to his skull, a critical detail that he believed should have been evident. After this revelation, the spirit ceased communicating.

In 1888 the old boarding house on Bond Street was torn down.

The Girl in the Well

On December 22, 1799, the narrow streets leading away from the heart of the city were coated in a thick layer of snow. Elma Sands, a young woman of modest means, had left her boarding house on Greenwich Street that evening, her spirits buoyed by the promise of elopement with Levi Weeks, a carpenter she had been dating. The cold was so piercing that she had borrowed a fur muff from a neighbor to protect her hands from the biting chill. Her destination remains a matter of speculation, but she vanished into the night, swallowed by the darkness and silence of the winter landscape.

When Elma failed to return, concern quickly morphed into dread. A search commenced, with the Hudson River being dragged in the grim hope of recovering her body. But the river yielded nothing, and hope began to wane with each passing day. It wasn't until two days after her disappearance that a glimmer of hope—or perhaps more accurately, a clue to her grim fate—emerged. Elma's fur muff was discovered about half a mile inland, an eerily silent witness lying near the fresh tracks of a one-horse sleigh. The muff was found not far from a well, a recent addition to the area, commissioned by the Manhattan Company.

This well was not just any structure; it was constructed with lumber and other materials purchased from Ezra Weeks, the brother of Levi Weeks. Located at 129 Spring Street, the well was an inconspicuous yet crucial piece of this macabre puzzle. In a twist of fate, the well into which

Elma Sands's body was ultimately discovered, preserved within the cold embrace of its waters.

The discovery of Elma's body in the well sparked outrage and grief, quickly followed by a thirst for justice. Levi Weeks was arrested and charged with her murder, setting the stage for what would become one of the most sensational trials of the early 19th century. The trial, held in 1800, was notable not only for its defendant and the tragic circumstances of the case but also for its legal representation. Levi Weeks was defended by none other than Alexander Hamilton and Aaron Burr, two of the era's most prominent figures, who would later find themselves on opposite sides of a duel that would end Hamilton's life.

The trial of Levi Weeks was a spectacle, drawing crowds eager to witness the drama unfold. Weeks insisted he was innocent and claimed that there had been an argument between the two on the night she was murdered, and he left her at the boarding house and went to see his brother. Despite the circumstantial evidence linking Weeks to the murder and testimony from 75 witnesses, the defense's skillful framing of Elma as promiscuous and suicidal combined with the lack of concrete evidence led to his acquittal. The verdict was met with shock and disbelief by those who were convinced of Weeks's guilt, but it marked the end of the legal proceedings, leaving the mystery of Elma Sands's death officially unsolved.

However, there are some who believe Levi Weeks may have been innocent all along. As the murder case was working its way through the court system. Another name was mentioned- Richard David Croucher.

Croucher was an English immigrant who had taken up residence in the boarding house where Elma Sands lived. He was known to be a somewhat unsavory character who liked to stealthily observe Levi Weeks and Elma being intimate.

Croucher's behavior before and after the murder drew significant attention. Known to have expressed a romantic interest in Elma Sands, Croucher's actions raised eyebrows. He was reported to have been overly familiar and somewhat aggressive in his advances towards Elma, which she apparently rebuffed.

On the night of her disappearance, several witnesses reported hearing arguments and unusual noises from the boarding house. Croucher's alibi was shaky, and his demeanor in the days following the murder was considered odd. He was reported to have spoken about the crime with a degree of familiarity and detail that some found disturbing. However, the authorities had their eyes on Weeks and never charged Croucher with murder. During the trial, Croucher raised some eyebrows by hastily marrying a local widow he barely knew. A month or two later, he was charged with raping his 13-year-old stepdaughter in the same boarding house. After agreeing to leave the state, Croucher was pardoned. He moved to Virigina and stayed for a while before moving back to England where he was executed for assaulting a woman.

Today, the well into which Elma Sands was found still

exists, hidden within the basement of a building at 129 Spring Street. Naturally, many believe the building is haunted.

According to those who work in the store, there have been many stories passed down over the years. Today, the spirits in the building seem mostly to enjoy messing with the elevator. The elevator often moves  between floors without being called and has become stuck on more than one occasion.

Tweed's Ghost

William Magear Tweed, commonly known as "Boss" Tweed, was an influential New York politician who rose to power in the mid-19th century. Born on April 3, 1823, in New York City, Tweed became the most powerful figure in the Tammany Hall political machine, which played a significant role in New York City politics.

Tweed's political career began in the 1850s when he was elected alderman. His big break came in 1863 when he was elected to the New York State Senate. As a senator, Tweed quickly leveraged his position to gain control over the Democratic Party in New York City, eventually becoming the Grand Sachem of Tammany Hall.

Originally established as a benevolent society for the city's burgeoning immigrant population, Tammany Hall transformed into a political powerhouse that controlled patronage and city contracts.

During the Civil War, Tweed became a

player in New York by working as an intermediary between poor immigrants and the government who were implementing conscription which led to the wildly unpopular military draft. By the late 1860s, Tweed had amassed an extraordinary amount of power and wealth through corrupt practices. He controlled the New York City government, the judiciary, and even had influence over the state legislature. His network of corruption involved embezzlement, bribery, and kickbacks. One of the most infamous examples of Tweed's corruption was the construction of the New York County Courthouse, commonly known as the Tweed Courthouse.

Tweed's influence over city contracts was unrivaled. He placed loyal cronies in key positions, ensuring that any contractor who wished to work on city projects had to play by his rules. Building the courthouse on Chambers Street became a golden opportunity to make a ton of money. Contractors who wanted a piece of the lucrative project submitted their bids, knowing that they would have to inflate their costs significantly.

Once the contracts were awarded, the contractors sent invoices to the city, often billing five or six times the actual cost of materials and labor. In fact, $250,000 in brooms were charged to the city. That number was the original cost of the entire building. Three tables and four charges cost the city nearly $180,000. Yet, city officials, many of whom were in Tweed's pocket, promptly approved these inflated invoices.

But the deceit didn't stop there. The contractors, having received their overpaid amounts from the city, were then required to return a substantial portion of the money as kickbacks to Tweed and his inner circle. This kickback system ensured that everyone involved in the conspiracy profited handsomely. The contractors got their cut, and Tweed and his cronies became wealthier.

Layer upon layer of bogus charges were added to the cost of the courthouse. Subcontractors, often in on the scheme, would add their own inflated costs, further driving up the bills sent to the city. Sometimes, invoices included charges for supplies and services that were never delivered. The city was paying for work that existed only on paper, while the funds were diverted into the pockets of the conspirators.

With key city officials under his thumb, Tweed ensured those inflated invoices were approved without scrutiny. Even officials who were not directly part of his inner circle were often bribed or intimidated into compliance. This manipulation and control over the city's finances created an almost impenetrable web of corruption.

As the courthouse project dragged on, its costs ballooned. What should have been a $250,000 construction turned into a staggering $13 million expense when it was finally completed in 1881. The public began to notice the discrepancies, and murmurs of corruption grew louder.

Journalists from The New York Times took up the mantle of investigation, digging into the labyrinthine financial records of the project. Meanwhile, political cartoonist Thomas Nast used his art to illustrate the extent of the corruption, his biting caricatures bringing the scandal to life for the city's residents.

The combination of hard-hitting journalism and poignant cartoons ignited public outrage. People demanded accountability, and the pressure mounted on those in power. Samuel J. Tilden, a determined lawyer and future governor, led the legal battle against Tweed. In 1871, the net finally closed around the corrupt boss. He was arrested and charged with multiple counts of forgery and larceny.

Tweed's trial in 1873 was a spectacle, drawing immense public interest. After the first trial ended in a hung jury, Tweed was convicted of 220 crimes including forgery and larceny. He was sentenced to twelve years in prison. However, after one year at the Tombs. His old nemesis (and current governor) Samuel Tilden was running for President and wanted to look tough on crime. He put pressure on the state attorney general to file a civil suit against Tweed to recoup $6 million that he had embezzled. Unable to make bail, he was placed in the Ludlow Street Jail.

Due to his connections, Tweed was allowed to leave the jail and return to his home on 5th Avenue to have dinner with his family. On December 4, 1875, Tweed didn't return to the jail after dinner. Instead, he slipped out a window where associates were waiting to whisk him away to New Jersey and then to Florida. Tweed eventually made his way to Havana, Cuba where he laid low for the summer of 1876 with his nephew, William Hunt. Once he learned that officials from the United States had learned of his whereabouts, he boarded a ship bound for Spain, hoping that the distance and lack of extradition treaties at the time would protect him from American law enforcement. Once in Vigo, Spain, Tweed adopted an alias of William Secor. Despite his efforts to remain inconspicuous, his distinctive appearance made it difficult for him to stay under the radar. Upon confirming his identity, Spanish officials arrested Tweed and extradited him back to the United States.

Upon his return, Tweed was re-incarcerated. His health declined rapidly in prison, and on April 12, 1878, he died in the Ludlow Street Jail. His life ended in disgrace, a stark contrast to the immense power and wealth he had once wielded.

Hauntings

Today, the Tweed Courthouse remains a prominent landmark in New York City. After undergoing extensive restorations in the late 20th century, it now serves as the headquarters for the New York City Department of Education. Its restoration preserved the building's historical integrity while adapting it for modern use. According to New York lore, Tweed's spirit haunts the old courthouse that he was so instrumental in building.

In the early 20th century, the old courthouse stood as a grand symbol of justice and civic duty. Its stately presence commanded respect by day, but by night, it transformed into a place of eerie mystery. The building's security guards, tasked with patrolling its vast and echoing halls, began to grow uneasy. Several guards quit their jobs, refusing to be in the courthouse after sundown. They spoke about hearing strange noises and seeing shadowy figures that seemed to move about the building. Among those who found themselves drawn into the courthouse's spectral lore was George Lyon, a jury clerk for the New York Supreme Court. Lyon was a practical man, who didn't believe in the supernatural, but his encounter with the courthouse's ghostly resident would challenge his skepticism.

One evening, Lyon had finished his dinner and returned to an empty courtroom. The jury had yet to reconvene, and he found himself with time to spare. He initially took a seat on one of the hard wooden benches, but the room was deserted, and he saw no harm in making himself more comfortable. He moved to the judge's chair, the most comfortable seat in the room.

Settling in, Lyon lit a cigar and began to scribble notes on his pad. The grand chandelier above cast a harsh, glaring light, so he decided to turn it off, preferring the soft glow of the streetlights filtering through the tall windows. Returning to the judge's chair, he propped his feet up on the desk and leaned back, enjoying the peace and quiet.

As he sat there in the dimly lit room, Lyon's relaxation was abruptly shattered. Out of the corner of his eye, he noticed a shadowy figure. It was the silhouette of a man, appearing in front of the mahogany door on the right side of the room. Lyon froze, his heart pounding as he watched the figure glide silently across the room. The apparition passed through the room and vanished through the closed door on the left side, disappearing as mysteriously as it had appeared.

Lyon's mind raced. He had heard the tales whispered among the courthouse staff—stories of the ghost of Bill Tweed, the infamous political boss who had once wielded immense power within these very walls. As much as Lyon wanted to dismiss these stories as mere superstition, the memory of the shadowy figure lingered.

In the weeks and months that followed, Lyon found himself returning to the courtroom, driven by a need to understand what he had seen. He sat in the judge's chair, retracing his steps and examining the room from every angle. He tried to convince himself that the figure had been a trick of the light, perhaps an electric streetlight casting an unusual shadow.

But over time, Lyon's skepticism waned. Each visit to the courtroom only deepened his conviction that he had witnessed something beyond explanation. The figure he had seen was no mere shadow; it was a ghost, a remnant of the courthouse's tumultuous past.

Native American Legends

The Curse of Lake Ronkonkoma

In the heart of Long Island lies Lake Ronkonkoma, a serene and picturesque body of water shrouded in mystery and legend. Among the most enduring and poignant tales is that of a Native American princess whose tragic story of love and heartbreak has been passed down through generations.

Princess Ronkonkoma was the daughter of the sachem, or chief, of the Setauket tribe. She was renowned for her beauty, grace, and kindness. Her people lived around the lake that now bears her name, and it was there that her fateful story unfolded.

As a young woman, Princess Ronkonkoma fell deeply in love with a European settler named Hugh Birdsall, who lived in a nearby village. Their love was forbidden, as the elders in the tribe didn't trust the European settlers.

Despite the obstacles, the princess and Birdsall would meet in secret by the water's edge, their love blossoming under the cover of darkness.

For a year, Princess Ronkonkoma and Hugh Birdsall maintained their secret romance. But the princess's father, the sachem, soon discovered their forbidden love. Angered and fearful of the repercussions from the elders in his tribe, he forbade Princess Ronkonkoma from seeing Birdsall and confined her to their village. Desperate to be with her beloved, the princess continued to row out to the center of the lake. Under the cover of darkness, she wrote a love letter to Birdsall on a piece of bark and then placed it in the water, gently nudging it until it began to float over towards Birdsall's camp.

At first she would find tree bark with letters from Birdsall almost every night in the lake. Then, over time, they dwindled until eventually it stopped altogether. It took a while, but eventually the princess figured out that Birdsall had left her and moved back home overseas to start a new life.

In a final act of despair, Princess Ronkonkoma rowed out to the center of the lake one night. There, she cried out to the Great Spirit, asking for deliverance from her pain and sorrow. According to legend, the princess tied her hair to a rock and stabbed herself in the heart as she flipped the boat over. Her body sank to the bottom of the lake and was never recovered.

After her suicide, the lake became a place of sorrow and mystery. It is said that every year, the spirit of Princess Ronkonkoma claims the life of a young man, drawing him into the lake's depths as a symbolic reunion with her lost love, Hugh Birdsall. This legend has fueled many stories of mysterious drownings at Lake Ronkonkoma.

The Fort Hill Haunting

During the Revolutionary War, there was a British fort along the bluffs of Oyster Bay, built to defend against Rochambeau's French fleet fighting on the side of the Colonists. This fort, initially named Fort Franklin, was later renamed Fort Hill. The fort was commanded by a young and handsome British officer named Captain Flanders.

One day, while walking through the woods outside the fort, Captain Flanders encountered a beautiful Indian girl, the daughter of a local chief named Tecumwah. It was love at first sight for Flanders, who became immediately smitten by her beauty. Driven by his infatuation, he abducted her and brought her back to the fort as a prisoner. Over time, the Indian Princess, who was initially resistant, fell in love with the charming British captain. She eventually agreed to stay with him, and Flanders renamed her Viola, a name she soon began to answer to.

Meanwhile, Chief Tecumwah, leader of the Wauwepek Indians who inhabited the area around the fort, searched tirelessly for his lost daughter, unaware that she was living only miles away within the confines of Fort Hill. One day, while traveling through the forest near Fort Hill, Tecumwah spotted his daughter and Captain Flanders holding hands and walking through the woods. Overcome with joy, he shouted to his daughter and rushed towards them. However, Flanders, realizing that this might be the young girl's father, grabbed Viola and sprinted back to the safety of the fort. Tecumwah, realizing he had been betrayed, stood outside the fort and vowed vengeance.

Determined to rescue his daughter, Tecumwah crossed the Long Island Sound and shared his story with a band of American soldiers based in Connecticut. The soldiers, already tasked with attacking Fort Hill, agreed to allow Tecumwah and his men to join them in the raid. Within days, boats launched from the shores of Connecticut under the cover of darkness, landing on the shores below Fort Hill. A vicious surprise attack ensued. The American forces, led by Tecumwah and his braves, soon breached the fort's walls and overwhelmed the outnumbered British forces.

As Tecumwah raced through the compound, now engulfed in flames, he saw his daughter standing beside Captain Flanders. With his tomahawk held high, Tecumwah charged towards them. Just as he was about to strike down Captain Flanders, Viola sprang in front of him to stop her father from killing her lover. Too late to halt his swing, Tecumwah's tomahawk accidentally decapitated his daughter.

In a blind rage, Flanders drew his sword and plunged it through Tecumwah's body, killing him instantly. The two lay side by side in the dirt, their tragic deaths a result of their love and loyalty.

Flanders was soon overwhelmed and taken prisoner by the American forces. Overcome with grief upon realizing he had not only lost Viola, but he had also killed her father, he broke free from his captors and drowned himself in a nearby lake.

According to legend, the woods around Fort Hill became haunted by the spirits of these three tragic individuals. Chief Tecumwah was said to search the forest in vain for his daughter's head. Captain Flanders was reported to search endlessly for the lost love of his life. Even eerier, villagers claimed to have seen the head of the Indian Princess rolling and bouncing through the forest in an endless search for her body.

Years later, a group of local teenagers went fishing in the area. After catching enough fish, they decided to cook their dinner. A young man named Alick Gadsden climbed the hill to the remains of Fort Hill to see the sunset. His friends, busy cooking, were startled by a blood-curdling scream and ran up the hill to find Alick hanging unconscious by his heels from the branches of a tree, naked with a corn cob in his mouth and strange hieroglyphics written all over his body in burnt cork.

Upon reviving, Alick recounted how he had seen a pack of what appeared to be ghostly natives inside the fort.

They had seized him, danced around him, and kicked him unmercifully before hanging him in the tree and disappearing like smoke.

Despite the legends, a wealthy lady named Mrs. Lloyd bought the property where the fort once stood and built a grand house with a cupola, naming it Fort Hill House. However, her husband knew of the legend and refused to move into his new home.

Ignoring warnings of hauntings, the headstrong Mrs. Lloyd moved in. However, she didn't stay long. Only after a few months in the mansion, she fled, claiming she had been chased out by spirits.

The house sat vacant for years and became known as a haunted house that the locals avoided.

Two brave sailors, intrigued by the legends, decided to investigate one night. They crawled through a window but quickly fled when they heard chains rattling and low moaning sounds. Their hasty departure out of the same window and subsequent retelling of the encounter added to the house's eerie legend. A few months later, a brave

Irish sailor named Pat McCabe took a bet to enter the haunted house alone. However, upon seeing something frightening in one of the windows, he tumbled down the hill in his haste to leave. The next morning, his hair had turned snow white from fright.

Years later, the Jesuits bought the property and cleansed the house of its spirits, facing no trouble thereafter.

Today, the house is gone, and no signs of its existence remain, but the legends of Fort Hill continue to haunt the imaginations of those who hear their tragic story.

Murder & Voodoo

Breaking the Hex

In the streets of Harlem in the 1920s, people gave the side-eye to Mary Johnson, a woman who had a reputation for faith healing and dabbling in the dark arts. Her strange rituals drew the curious and desperate to her apartment at 168 East 110th Street. Her practices, rooted in the traditions of voodoo, offered unconventional solutions to those beleaguered by ailments and troubles beyond the realm of modern medicine. Yet, within the walls of their home, Mary's husband, Nathaniel Conway, harbored deep reservations about her forays into the supernatural. A devout Christian, Nathaniel's faith stood in stark contrast to Mary's beliefs, sowing discord and tension between them.

On February 24, 1929, Nathaniel's simmering discontent reached a boiling point. Convinced beyond reason that Mary was casting spells upon him, and that divine intervention demanded he put an end to her voodoo practices, an argument erupted. Words gave way to violence, and the domestic dispute spiraled out of control. The commotion caught the attention of a neighbor, who, upon hearing Mary's desperate screams, rushed to find help. In a stroke of fate, they encountered patrolman Harold Bergman on the street.

Guided by the echoes of distress, Officer Bergman hurried to the apartment. The scene that greeted him upon entry was one of chaos and violence: Nathaniel, in a frenzied state, was choking Mary and stabbing her mercilessly with a knife. Caught in the act, Nathaniel

hurled an empty milk bottle at the officer in a futile
attempt at defense.

Bergman, faced with no other choice, drew his pistol and
discharged two shots. The bullets found their mark,
injuring Nathaniel on the right side of his head and his
right wrist, effectively halting the assault.

Nathaniel was rushed to the hospital, where his wounds
were treated urgently. Once stable, he was taken to the
East 104th police station for interrogation. The gravity of
his actions began to dawn on him as he rambled
incoherently, claiming to have been carrying out the
Lord's work, weary of being ensnared by his wife's hexes

that compelled him to partake in voodoo ceremonies against his will.

Tragically, Mary succumbed to her injuries. Nathaniel, now a murderer in the eyes of the law, faced justice for his heinous act. His ramblings and erratic behavior led to his confinement in an insane asylum, where he spent the rest of his life.

The Dark Prophecy

Anna and Tomas Casiano were Puerto Rican immigrants who had moved to New York City with dreams of building a better life. Their niche was carved out through their practices of voodoo, catering to locals that sought spiritual guidance and mystical remedies. Anna, a gifted spiritualist, performed private fortune-telling sessions in their home on Fulton Avenue, attracting a growing list of clients. Meanwhile, Tomas capitalized on her clientele by selling voodoo dolls, statues, herbs, and candles. Business thrived, and Tomas eventually opened a small store around the corner on Third Avenue to accommodate the increasing demand.

In the fall of 1962, Anna received a chilling vision. She foresaw the death of her husband. The vision left her deeply shaken, and she rushed to Tomas, tears streaming down her face, begging him to leave New York and return to Puerto Rico. Tomas, ever the skeptic and always reassuring, comforted her. He told her not to worry, insisting that he would be fine.

A few weeks later, Tomas hired a man named Pedro Ramos Pagan to help around the store. Pagan served as a clerk and handyman, assisting with the day-to-day operations. However, as winter approached, business began to falter. Tomas struggled to pay Pagan consistently, giving him what he could but often falling short. Frustrated and feeling undervalued, Pagan eventually quit.

In early November, Pagan stopped by the shop and demanded the $12 Tomas owed him. Tomas, strapped for cash, promised to pay him if he came back in a few days. On November 9, Pagan went to Tomas' house, again demanding his money. Tomas, late for work and with no cash on hand, pushed past Pagan and began walking briskly to his store just around the corner. Pagan, feeling disrespected and increasingly aggravated, followed him. The two men argued as they walked the streets, their voices rising with each step.

Upon reaching the store, Pagan's anger was boiling over as he barged inside behind Tomas. He began rummaging through the shelves, looking for something valuable to take as repayment. As he cursed Tomas, he picked up a plaster statue and proceeded to walk out of the store with it. Tomas, pushed to his limit, swung and hit Pagan in the face.

In a rage, Pagan violently smashed the statue over Tomas' head, stunning him. Tomas quickly recovered and lunged at Pagan, initiating a brutal grappling match inside the store. They wrestled furiously, knocking over shelves and smashing fixtures, destroying merchandise in the chaos.

Tomas managed to get on top of Pagan and began pummeling him. Desperate and seeing no other way out, Pagan reached into his pocket and pulled out a four-inch screwdriver. With a surge of adrenaline, he began stabbing Tomas repeatedly in the stomach. Tomas collapsed, but Pagan, driven by a mix of fear and fury,

stabbed him three more times in the back before fleeing the scene.

An hour later, the landlord, concerned about the noise, came by to check on Tomas. Opening the door, she was horrified to find the aftermath of the violent struggle and Tomas lying in a pool of blood. She ran to call the police, and when medical personnel arrived, they pronounced Tomas dead. The official cause of death was a punctured lung, fulfilling the grim prophecy Anna had foreseen.

Pedro Ramos Pagan was arrested two days later and charged with murder. In court, he claimed self-defense, but the severity of his actions led to a lengthy prison sentence. However, he was released for good behavior in January 1971.

Yet, fate had one final twist. A few weeks later on February 13, 1971, while crossing Prospect Avenue,

Pagan was struck by a car and died on the way to the hospital.

The eerie coincidence led to whispers and rumors throughout New York City. According to local lore, Pagan had been cursed by the Casiano family, and his untimely death was seen as the inevitable fulfillment of that curse.

New, Old Ghost Stories

In early February 1866, Philadelphia, Pennsylvania was abuzz with rumors of a sinister specter wreaking havoc in a large house on South Fifth Street. The eerie tale quickly gained traction, capturing the attention of the entire city and making headlines in The Philadelphia Inquirer the very next day.

The ghostly narrative gripped Philadelphia, plunging its residents into a state of collective hysteria. Such was the fervor that the Inquirer, overwhelmed by demand, found itself compelled to issue an apology in a subsequent edition for failing to print sufficient copies of the paper that chronicled the haunting on South Fifth Street. The article revealed that by mid-morning, newsstands were bereft of any remaining copies, prompting Philadelphians to lend their copies to neighbors or sell them on the streets.

However, it eventually emerged that the entire affair had been an elaborate ruse orchestrated by a foster child. Nonetheless, the Inquirer capitalized on the situation, generating sensationalized headlines for a remarkable span of six consecutive days.

You know the old saying, "If it bleeds, it leads"? Well, in the United States in the late 19th century you could say, "If it's haunted, it's wanted."

By the 1890s newspapers from all over the country including New York were putting tales of local hauntings on the front page every month or so. Today we have the term "clickbait", but back then newspaper editors knew that if they ran a ghost story, readers would flock to the newsstands, and they would sell more papers. Naturally, this led to more revenue for the paper as well as increased salary for the staff and editor.

Not every ghost story that was featured in the local newspapers turned out to be legitimate. A lot of times, after a day or so, the haunting could be proven to be a hoax. But many could not be debunked.

Here is a collection of some of the most noteworthy New York City ghost stories that have long been forgotten.

The Haunting on East 55th Street

In the spring of 1892, the air in New York City was thick with the promise of new beginnings. Virginia Adler and her husband, Raymond, welcomed their newborn son into the world. Seeking a fresh start for their growing family, they moved into a larger flat on the second floor of a building on East 55th Street. The couple, filled with hope and anticipation, believed this was the perfect place to raise their child.

However, their peace was short-lived. Almost immediately after moving in, Virginia began to hear strange sounds at night. Initially, she dismissed them as the creaks and groans of an unfamiliar building settling. But one night, the noises became impossible to ignore. Awakened by the sound of heavy footsteps pacing around her bed, Virginia's heart raced. She glanced over to see Raymond sleeping soundly beside her, his rhythmic snoring undisturbed by the noise. Terrified, she shook him awake.

"It's just the servant," Raymond mumbled, trying to reassure her. They had recently hired a young woman to help care for their baby, and Raymond was certain she was the source of the disturbance. But when Virginia checked the servant's room, she found her sound asleep, unfazed by any noise.

Raymond quickly fell back asleep, but an anxious Virginia remained wide awake, her mind racing. As she lay there, a strange, bright light appeared in the room. It floated inches from her face, damp and shimmering, sprinkling water on her skin. Paralyzed with fear, she couldn't move or scream.

The light hovered for a few minutes before disappearing, leaving Virginia shaken and unable to sleep.

For several nights, the eerie occurrences continued. Virginia, not wanting to burden her already overworked husband, kept her fears to herself. Raymond worked long hours at a nearby slaughterhouse, and she didn't want to add to his stress. But the strange events persisted, and eventually, Virginia confided in Raymond that she believed their home was haunted.

Raymond admitted that he too had seen the mysterious light in their bedroom. Together, they decided to act. Virginia's two brothers and their cousin William were invited to stay at the flat to witness the strange events for themselves.

That night, the men settled into different rooms, prepared to face whatever came. At around 2 a.m., a cold wind swept through the house, strong enough to open doors.

The bright light reappeared, this time in William's room. It hovered before his face, and when he reached his hand out to touch it, he was rendered unconscious.

Virginia's brothers rushed to his side, finding him pale and unresponsive. They shook him until he regained consciousness, his eyes wide with fear.

The following day, the Adlers decided they could no longer stay in the flat. However, Virginia's brothers were determined to uncover the truth. They returned the next night, ready to confront whatever haunted the house. As darkness fell, the eerie noises began again. Suddenly, a window flew open, seemingly lifted by unseen hands.

The brothers were convinced more than ever that the house was haunted.

News of the haunting spread quickly, eventually making its way to the local newspapers. The landlord, Joseph Merrin, vehemently denied any supernatural activity, claiming the Adlers simply could not afford their rent. Despite his assertions, the Adlers, along with Virginia's brothers and cousin, stood firm in their belief that a ghost haunted the building.

The mystery of the East 55th Street faded in time and new tenants eventually moved in. There were no other reports of the alleged haunting.

The Mapleton Mystery

In the early morning hours of August 5, 1894, people in Mapleton were shocked by an eerie discovery. A watchman, making his routine rounds near the Mapleton train station, stumbled upon a sight that would haunt him for years to come. In a small clearing, he saw what appeared to be a woman asleep. As he approached to rouse her and send her home, he was horrified to find her covered in blood. Panic set in as he quickly realized the woman was dead.

Shaking, he covered her with a white sheet, weighing it down with small stones, and ran to get help.

When the sun rose the following morning, the coroner arrived at the scene and quickly ruled the death a suicide. The woman had apparently shot herself through the heart with a pistol that lay beside her. Her body was taken to the morgue, where it was hoped someone would come to claim her.

Two days later, Helena Barning received an anonymous letter containing a clipping from the Evening World about the suicide, and she feared the worst. The dead woman might be her sister-in-law, Margaret Barning, a pretty 26-year-old who had been missing for several days.

Margaret's family was bewildered. Despite Helena's medical issues, she had a steady job at a rope factory and had friends in her boarding house on Hanson Place. The other boarders mentioned she had been seeing an older man who frequently visited. Despite the family's protests, the authorities dismissed the case as a suicide of a poor woman, unwilling to investigate further.

On August 9, Margaret was laid to rest in Jersey City Cemetery. However, her soul would not rest in peace. Rumors soon spread of a ghostly woman floating across the field where her body was discovered.

Crowds gathered nightly, hoping to glimpse the apparition. The watchman who found her body even placed a large white stone at the site to mark it for curious onlookers.

On August 14, eight armed servicemen

camped out in the field, intent on capturing the ghost. Yet, night after night, the spectral woman failed to appear, and the crowds dwindled. Just as interest waned, a white ghostly form was seen again, this time by a railroad flagman. The news reignited the ghost fever, and crowds returned in droves.

A group of firefighters from the nearby Windsor Hose Company decided to take matters into their own hands. They rushed towards the ghost one night, only to discover it was a cleverly rigged contraption: 2x4s and a white sheet attached to a wire. The mastermind behind the hoax was never found.

Although the ghost was exposed as a hoax, whispers of hauntings persisted. Locals claimed to see shadows and lights in the field, convinced Margaret's spirit still roamed.

On the night of August 5, 1895, exactly one year after the tragic discovery of Margaret Barning's body, John Hennessey lay in his quarters on the Lott estate, trying to go to sleep. Suddenly, he heard a faint tapping at his window. Hennessey, half-asleep, initially dismissed it as the wind or some birds pecking against the glass. As the tapping persisted, however, it grew louder and more insistent, pulling him from his drowsiness. The sound was almost rhythmic, like a deliberate knock meant to wake him. Sitting up in bed, he strained to see through the darkness, but the window revealed nothing out of the ordinary.

Curiosity piqued, Hennessey rose and moved to the window, cautiously pulling back the curtain. The night was calm, the moon casting a silvery glow over the field behind his dwelling. There was no sign of anything that could have caused the noise. He opened the window and looked around, but still, there was nothing. With a furrowed brow, he closed the window and returned to bed, the tapping sound now silent.

Meanwhile, across the field near the Mapleton train station, a group of late-night travelers on a train from Coney Island experienced their own strange encounter. As the train passed through the field, several passengers claimed to see a ghostly figure in white drifting from the Lott estate where John Hennessey had been sleeping. The figure, eerily similar to the descriptions of Margaret's apparition, moved silently across the ground, disappearing into the woods. The passengers, wide-eyed and whispering among themselves, spread the story quickly,

reigniting the ghostly legend.

That same night, two servant girls at Michael McCormack's house near the train station were jolted awake by the sound of a train whistle. As they looked out their window, they too saw a spectral woman in a white dress skimming across the ground with an unnatural speed. Their frightened screams echoed through the house, waking the other occupants, but by the time that anyone else looked, the apparition was gone.

The following evening, Mary Erdman, a passenger on a late-night train, saw something emerge from the woods. She was so terrified by the sight of a tall, silent figure in white that she fainted in the arms of a nearby policeman. She later recounted her experience to a reporter from the Evening World, "I saw it. I don't believe in ghosts, not one bit, and I don't say I saw a ghost. But I did see something all in white, tall and silently gliding along and I actually fainted from fright. I never again expect to stay for that late train because the doctor said I can't stand severe shocks."

Around midnight that night, laborer Mike Clooch, also experienced something. While working on a Sea Beach Railway train, Clooch screamed in horror when he saw a glowing, translucent woman floating across the field. He and his fellow workers, paralyzed by fear, hid in the engineer's cab and begged to be taken back to the station.

An hour later, conductor Michael Hilder watched in disbelief as the spectral figure emerged from the woods and glided across the train tracks in front of him.

Days later, conductor Thomas Tully encountered the supposed ghost, which upon closer inspection, turned out to be a stray pig. This revelation cast doubt on the previous sightings, suggesting they might have been cases of mistaken identity.

Despite Tully's rational explanation, the tales of Margaret's ghost persisted. Whether it was a ghost or pig, it remained an enduring mystery for over a year until the sightings finally subsided.

The Last Voyage of the Townsend

In the mid-19th century, Uriah Sears, a seasoned and hard-nosed sailor, commissioned the construction of a two-masted schooner in Poughkeepsie, New York. He named the ship "Adelaide Townsend" in honor of his beloved wife, Adelaide, who was not only his wife but also an integral member of his crew. Their partnership was personal and professional, marked by a mutual love for the sea. The couple's wedding day took place the same day the ship was launched, reflecting their intertwined destinies.

Captain Sears and Adelaide embarked on their maiden voyage to Scotland, carrying young John H. Hogan, a 22-year-old deckhand, alongside them. Upon their return, the schooner commenced regular journeys along the Atlantic seaboard, transporting cordwood and other goods between New York City and Virginia, and occasionally venturing as far as the West Indies to transport rum and sugar.

Tragedy struck shortly after these voyages began. During a fierce storm, one of the ship's sails became untethered. As the crew worked frantically to pull down the thrashing sail, a colossal wave struck the Townsend with devastating force. The impact was so powerful that it ripped one of the ship's two masts clean off. The mast's fall created a domino effect of chaos and destruction, scattering debris across the deck and severely compromising the ship's stability.

At this critical moment, Adelaide was near the ship's edge, trying her best to hold on. The combination of the mast falling, the ship's violent lurch, and the overwhelming force of water was catastrophic. Adelaide was swept overboard by the massive wave, pulled away into the rolling sea.

Despite immediate efforts to save her, the storm made rescue attempts nearly impossible. The darkness, intensified by the storm's heavy rain and spray, along with the tumultuous waves hampered the crew's efforts to locate her.

Despite the crew's efforts to save Adelaide, she was lost to the ocean's depths. The loss devastated Captain Sears, casting a shadow of sorrow over him that darkened the remainder of the voyage.

The grief-stricken captain fell into a deep depression, a state from which he only partially recovered on the journey back to New York. His once jovial nature was shattered, and a few months later, while en route to Jamaica, he succumbed to tuberculosis. In his final moments, in the sweltering heat of his cabin in Kingston Harbor, Captain Sears made a promise to John Hogan. He bequeathed the "Adelaide Townsend" to the young sailor, making him swear never to let anyone else captain the ship as long as he lived. Mysteriously, he whispered, "I'll be back to see that you never let anybody else sail her," before rolling over and drawing his last breath.

Hogan, now Captain Hogan, honored Sears's last wishes and took command of the schooner. He soon discovered that the ship was haunted by more than just the former captain's memories. Crew members reported hearing unexplained voices and seeing strange phenomena, such as a mysterious blue light in Hogan's cabin and sightings of Sears sitting solemnly on his bunk.

These strange occurrences were most frequent in warmer waters, perhaps stirred by the same tropical climates Sears had loved. Despite the eerie manifestations, Hogan found comfort in these signs, believing that Sears's spirit was watching over him and the ship.

However, maintaining a crew proved challenging, as sailors were often frightened away by the supernatural events, abandoning ship as soon as it docked. The locals mocked the old patched-together vessel, but Hogan remained steadfast, convinced that Sears' presence kept the schooner afloat.

As the years wore on, Hogan's physical condition deteriorated. By 1908, crippled with arthritis and aged 73, he reluctantly decided to hand over the helm of Captain Sears' ship to another captain for a winter voyage. This decision would lead to disaster. On January 13, 1909, under the command of Captain Henry Thornblem, the "Adelaide Townsend" was struck by a steamboat in a storm off the Delaware capes and tragically sank, taking Thornblem and several crew members down with it.

The wreckage of the schooner washed ashore the next day, identified by pieces of Hogan's wooden trunk. Overwhelmed by guilt and heartache, Hogan believed that breaking his promise to Sears had doomed the ship.

He lived out his remaining days haunted by regret, convinced that his failure to abide by his promise had led to the schooner's demise, fulfilling the eerie prophecy left by Sears in his dying breath.

Angelina's Last Ride

In the summer of 1936, the streets of Manhattan buzzed not just with the usual hum of city life but with whispers of the supernatural, thanks to the audacious challenge issued by Joseph Dunninger. Dunninger, a celebrated stage magician and the then-president of the Universal Council for Psychic Research, had long been a vocal skeptic of the paranormal. His bold proclamation splashed across the local newspapers, offering a jaw-dropping $10,000 reward to anyone who could present him with indisputable proof of an apparition—a challenge he believed no one could meet.

The stage for this eerie challenge was an unassuming, rundown apartment building on East 86th Street, a place shrouded in dark rumors and tragic histories. Among its grim tales was that of Angelina, a woman whose life had been gunned down in a drunken rage by her husband in 1917. In the years following her untimely death, tenants and neighbors whispered of sightings of Angelina's spirit, clad in a spectral blue or white dress.

Eager to confront these rumors head-on, Dunninger struck a deal with the building's superintendent, Leo Markowsky, arranging to spend the night inside the supposed haunted apartment alongside H. S. Pretty, a former resident who claimed to have encountered the ghostly figure of Angelina on multiple occasions. Dunninger promised Pretty the money should a ghost appear during their vigil.

On the night of July 29th, the building brimmed with anticipation as Dunninger, Pretty, and a contingent of off-duty police officers settled in for the night. Yet, as hours ticked by, the group encountered nothing out of the ordinary — no signs of the ethereal lady in white who had become the subject of so much local lore.

The calm of the vigil was shattered when Everett Davidson, a young salesman drawn to the building by the swirling rumors, snuck into the apartment. His

sudden screams for help pierced the night, drawing the officers to his aid. Davidson, wild-eyed, pointed towards a window where he claimed the apparition of Angelina was materializing. Yet, the supposed ghostly scene was quickly rationalized by the officers as nothing more than the interplay of external lights from a nearby building casting eerie shadows.

Days later, the story took another turn when a passerby, walking with friends along 86th Street, fainted at the sight of a luminous-faced woman in white staring down from the third floor. Despite an extensive investigation by the police and reporters, no evidence of the ghostly figure was found.

As the story made headlines, people flocked to East 86th Street to see if they could see the ghost for themselves.

After a few days went by with no sightings, the mystery deepened when taxi driver Jack Bradley came forward with a tale that seemed to straddle the line between reality and the otherworldly. According to Bradley, a mysterious woman in black had hailed his cab in front of the building, requesting a ride over the Queensboro Bridge to the nearest cemetery.

Strangely, upon reaching her destination, the woman vanished in the backseat of the cab, leaving no trace behind but a chilled, unnerved driver.

After that night, Angelina was no longer seen in the old apartment building. Some speculated that the taxi ride across the Queensboro Bridge was her final departure from the neighborhood that had been the stage for her posthumous fame.

The building that once stood as a silent witness to these mysteries was eventually demolished, replaced by a new structure in 1939.

Historical Hauntings

The New Amsterdam Theatre

Located at 214 West 42nd Street, the New Amsterdam Theatre stands as a monumental piece of theatrical and architectural history. Since its opening in 1903, the New Amsterdam has been an emblem of the artistic glamour and architectural grandeur of the early 20th century.

The New Amsterdam Theatre was designed by the noted architectural firm Herts and Tallant, known for their specialization in theatre designs. The theatre was one of the first in New York to be built with a steel-framed structure and was considered the most opulent facility of its time.

The New Amsterdam's façade and interiors were adorned with intricate designs, including floral and organic forms, which were typical of Art Nouveau. Its use of stained glass, ornamental ironwork, and plush seating added to the overall effect of luxury and modernity.

The theatre opened in November 1903 with a production of "A Midsummer Night's Dream." However, it is perhaps best known for its association with impresario Florenz Ziegfeld. From 1913 to 1937, the New Amsterdam Theatre hosted the famous Ziegfeld Follies, a series of lavish musical revues that epitomized the glamour of the era and featured stars such as Fred Astaire, Bob Hope, Fanny Brice, Bert Williams, and Will Rogers.

Following the Great Depression, the theatre's fortunes declined along with the economy. The rise of motion pictures also contributed to its difficulties. By the 1930s, the New Amsterdam had shifted from live theatre to become a movie house and vaudeville shows. Over the next few decades, the building fell into disrepair, and by the late 1970s and early 1980s, it was largely abandoned, reflecting the general decline of Times Square during this period.

In the mid-1990s, a major restoration project was undertaken by The Walt Disney Company in partnership with the City and State of New York, as part of a broader initiative to revitalize the Times Square area. The restoration, completed in 1997, aimed to return the theatre to its original grandeur while updating it for modern productions.

Disney's restoration included meticulous attention to historical detail, refurbishing the ornate interiors and façade and updating the building's infrastructure. The theatre reopened on May 18, 1997, with the premiere of Disney's musical "King David" and later became the flagship venue for the hugely successful "The Lion King," which ran there until 2006 before moving to the Minskoff Theatre.

Today, the New Amsterdam Theatre continues to be a vital part of New York City's cultural landscape, hosting popular Broadway shows under the management of Disney Theatrical Productions.

Hauntings

The ghost of Olive Thomas is one of the most storied and enduring legends of the New Amsterdam Theatre. Olive was a rising star of the Ziegfeld Follies and silent film actress whose tragic death at the age of 25 has left a haunting legacy.

Olive Thomas was born Olive Duffy in 1894 in Charleroi, Pennsylvania. She moved to New York City in her late teens and quickly became a popular model. Her beauty and charisma led her to the stages of Broadway, where she caught the eye of Florenz Ziegfeld, who cast her in his infamous Ziegfeld Follies. Thomas's charm and talent made her a standout in the shows, and she quickly transitioned to silent films, becoming a celebrated star of the early silver screen.

Her life took a glamorous yet tumultuous turn when she married Jack Pickford, the younger brother of silent film superstar Mary Pickford, in 1916. The couple was known for their lavish lifestyle and headline-making antics, embodying the Roaring Twenties' spirit of excess. However, their marriage was marked by intense highs and lows, fueled by both passion and partying.

In September 1920, while vacationing in Paris, Olive Thomas died under mysterious circumstances. The official cause of death was acute nephritis following a supposed accidental poisoning by ingesting a lethal dose of mercury bichloride. Her death was ruled accidental, but rumors persisted that she was depressed and chose to end her life. Olive's body was shipped back to New York aboard the Mauretania and she was laid to rest at Woodlawn Cemetery.

Three weeks after Olive's death a silent film she had shot earlier in the year, "Everybody's Sweetheart" was released on October 4.

To honor her legacy, the New Amsterdam Theatre hung a photograph of her on a wall in the cafeteria. However, after dozens of patrons tried to steal it, the picture was taken down.

Since her untimely death, numerous accounts have emerged of Olive's ghost haunting the theatre, particularly around the area where the Ziegfeld Follies girls' dressing rooms were located. She is most often seen after the theatre empties, by custodians or by actors working late.

The most commonly reported sighting describes Olive as appearing in a beautiful green beaded dress, similar to one she wore in the Follies, carrying a blue glass bottle. Witnesses report that she seems to be eternally performing, dancing and fluttering across the stage and through the corridors with a playful, if not melancholic, demeanor.

Employees of the New Amsterdam Theatre are well aware of Olive's presence and have come to regard her as an integral part of the theatre's community. New staff members are often jokingly warned to "be nice to Olive," indicating her accepted and somewhat beloved status among the theatre's regulars who also acknowledge her with greetings when they arrive and before leaving.

Disney's restoration of the New Amsterdam Theatre in the late 1990s seemed to intensify sightings of Olive Thomas's spirit. During renovations, workers reportedly encountered her, with some claiming that she was observing the changes and ensuring that they were respectful to the history of the place she loved. One evening as a contractor was about to leave for the night, he heard a lady behind him call out, "How are you doing, handsome?" When he turned around no one was there.

The Empire State Building

The Empire State Building, an iconic symbol of New York City and a marvel of modern engineering, has a rich history that spans nearly a century.

However, before the skyscraper became a staple of the skyline, the prime real estate on Fifth Avenue originally belonged to two hotels, the Waldorf and the Astoria. The hotels were built by feuding cousins William Waldorf Astor and John Jacob Astor IV in 1893 and 1897 respectively. The cousins finally agreed to bury the hatchet and the two buildings were connected through a 300-foot marble corridor known as Peacock Alley. The Waldorf-Astoria set a new standard for service and luxury, establishing itself as the social center for New York's elite.

The idea for the Empire State Building was born during the late 1920s, a time of fierce competition among New York City's builders to construct the world's tallest skyscraper. The project was spearheaded by John J. Raskob, a former vice president of General Motors, and Alfred E. Smith, a former New York governor. They envisioned a towering structure that would surpass the height of the Chrysler Building, which was then under construction and vying for the title of the world's tallest building.

The architectural firm of Shreve, Lamb & Harmon Associates was commissioned to design the building. Architect William F. Lamb, drawing on previous experience with the Reynolds Building in Winston-Salem, North Carolina, conceptualized the Empire State Building's distinctive Art Deco design. The final plans called for a 1,250-foot-tall building with 102 floors, designed to house a variety of commercial offices.

Construction of the Empire State Building began on March 17, 1930, and was completed in a staggering 410 days, with the building officially opening on May 1, 1931. The rapid construction pace was achieved through the use of advanced building techniques and the labor of over 3,400 workers, many of whom were immigrants and Mohawk ironworkers from Canada. Despite the dangers of unspeakable heights and hot rivets literally flying around the construction site, the project was completed with a relatively low number of fatalities for such a large-scale endeavor — officially five workers died during construction.

The building's structure consists of a steel frame with limestone and granite cladding, giving it both strength and aesthetic appeal. One of the engineering marvels of

the Empire State Building is its foundation, which had to support the immense weight of the building. Engineers dug deep into Manhattan's bedrock to anchor the foundation securely.

Upon its completion, the Empire State Building surpassed the Chrysler Building and became the tallest building in the world, a title it held for nearly 40 years until the completion of the World Trade Center's North Tower in 1970. The building's opening coincided with the Great Depression, leading to a slow initial occupancy rate, earning it the nickname "Empty State Building." However, its observation deck and breathtaking views of New York City became an immediate hit, attracting visitors from all over the world and providing a steady source of income.

The Empire State Building quickly became a cultural icon. It has appeared in numerous films, most famously in the 1933 classic "King Kong," where the giant ape climbs to the top of the building. This image cemented the building's place in popular culture. Over the years, it has been featured in various other movies, television shows, and books, symbolizing New York City itself.

The Empire State Building was originally conceived with an ambitious plan to include a mooring mast for airships at its pinnacle. This idea was a product of the 1920s, an era fascinated with the potential of air travel, particularly via lighter-than-air craft like blimps and zeppelins. The proposal envisioned the building as a practical and futuristic transportation hub that would serve not only as the world's tallest skyscraper but also as a gateway for transatlantic airship travel.

The idea was that airships would moor at the mast, and passengers would disembark via a gangplank extending from the airship to a door on the 102nd floor of the building.

Despite the visionary nature of this plan, several practical challenges soon became evident. One of the primary issues was the strong and unpredictable winds at such high altitudes, which made it extremely difficult to safely maneuver and secure a large airship. Additionally, the wind around the skyscraper was turbulent and dangerous, posing significant risks to both the airships and the building itself.

Another challenge was the lack of infrastructure for handling passengers and cargo in a manner that would be efficient and safe. There was also concern about the potential fire hazards associated with hydrogen-filled airships, a danger that became tragically apparent with the Hindenburg disaster in 1937.

In September 1931, a small dirigible, the Goodyear Blimp Columbia, attempted a mooring at the Empire State Building's mast. In an attempt to pick up two bags of mail, the blimp flew past the tower twelve times. However, it couldn't get close enough to the mooring mast and wasn't able to stay stable in the high-altitude winds. The test was short-lived, and the plan was ultimately deemed impractical and abandoned. The mast, originally designed as a docking station, was never used for its intended purpose.

The Plane Crash

On Saturday, July 25, 1945, Lieutenant Colonel William F. Smith was flying a Mitchell B-25 twin engine bomber on a routine personnel transport mission from Bedford Army Airfield in Massachusetts to Newark Airport in New Jersey. Weather conditions were poor, with heavy fog shrouding New York City, reducing visibility significantly.

Despite being advised to divert to another airport due to the inclement weather, Lt. Col. Smith continued his approach. As he neared New York City, the dense fog obscured his vision, and he became disoriented. Around 9:40 a.m., as the bomber flew over Manhattan, Smith, unaware of his proximity to the skyscrapers, attempted to navigate through the fog.

The B-25 crashed into the north side of the Empire State Building at 9:49 a.m., between the 78th and 80th floors. The impact from the ten-ton plane created a massive explosion, with debris and flames engulfing the building's upper floors. The explosion caused a hole about 18 feet wide and 20 feet high in the facade, while one of the engines shot through the building and exited from the south side, landing on the roof of a nearby building, starting a fire there as well.

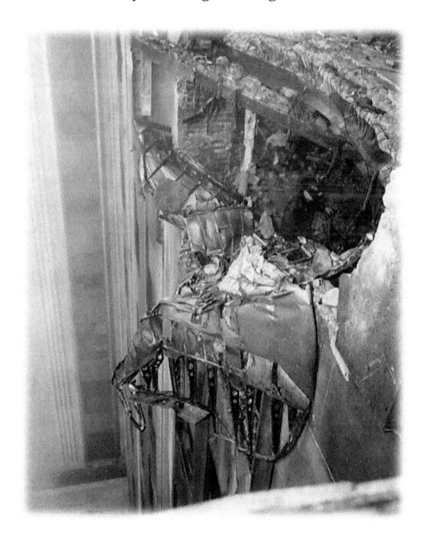

The crash killed all three crew members aboard the bomber: Lt. Col. Smith, Staff Sergeant Christopher Domitrovich, and an enlisted man named Albert Perna.

19-year-old Lucille Bath was one of the eleven people who just happened to be in the wrong place at the wrong time. Though she was on vacation from her job working for the National Catholic Welfare Conference, she went in that morning after her boss told her that they were shorthanded. She perished that day in her office on the 79th floor along with nine of her coworkers.

Betty Lou Oliver, an elevator operator survived the initial impact only to fall 75 stories in an elevator when the cables snapped due to the explosion. Remarkably, she survived this fall, setting a Guinness World Record for the longest survived elevator fall.

Emergency responders quickly arrived at the scene. Firefighters bravely battled the blaze, which was compounded by the high altitude and strong winds at that level. The fire was brought under control within 40 minutes, preventing further casualties and damage. The skyscraper suffered no structural damage and was reopened just two days later.

Jumpers

A few weeks before the Empire State Building officially opened, the first suicide took place. With no more work to be done on the massive skyscraper, Fred Egland, a 45-year-old workman from Brooklyn was told he was being let go. Not knowing what to do next, he climbed to the 78th floor and jumped into an elevator shaft. His remains were found on the 21st floor.

Nevertheless, Egland's death wouldn't be the last on the site. On November 3, 1932, an unassuming German man in his 30s wearing a gray suit with a blue tie paid $1.10 to visit the observation tower on the 86th floor. In the elevator, building security noticed that he appeared to be nervous. Thinking that their guest had a fear of heights, they thought little of it but still took him to the 102nd floor to get a better view. As soon as the elevator opened, the man darted out and ran up some stairs to the 103rd floor of the building which was off limits to visitors. A guard on the 102nd floor noticed the visitor and took off after him. However, before he could be caught, the man hopped a rail and jumped. His body landed on the roof of the 86th floor observation deck rest room.

Over the next decade a handful of people tried to jump from the observation deck but were apprehended before they could make the tragic leap. But that all changed on July 7, 1946, when Charles Vogel, an ailing retired night elevator operator spent his last $1.20 to buy a ticket to the observation deck on the 86th floor. When security personnel weren't looking, Vogel jumped from the observation deck. However, the wind knocked him back against the building and he only fell to the 85th floor below. Vogel seemed to have injured his leg and couldn't stand. So, in his desperation to end his life, Charles Vogel crawled to the ledge and hurled himself off of it. He fell 55 stories and landed on a setback on the 30th floor.

Ten months later, a similar situation unfolded on May 9, 1947. Solomon Rossbach, a 54-year-old down on his luck diamond dealer jumped from the observation deck. Like Charles Vogel, Rossbach landed on the ledge of the 85th floor. Guards rushed out to help him, but before they could reach him, he hurled himself over the ledge. His twisted remains were found on the same 30th floor setback.

The most infamous suicide that took place at the Empire State Building also happened that same month. Evelyn McHale was a 23-year-old Long Island bookkeeper who seemed to have a lot to live for. She was engaged to Barry Rhodes, a Pennsylvania college student and the couple appeared to be happy. In fact, on the morning of May 1, Evelyn visited her fiancée and seemed to be in good spirits. Unbeknownst to him, after Evelyn left his side and took the train back to New York, she went straight to the Empire State Building, and bought a ticket to the observation deck.

Around 10:40 a.m., Evelyn leapt with such force that she cleared the parapet of the 17th and 5th floors. She fell more than a thousand feet and landed on the roof of an unoccupied United Nations limousine parked at the curb on Fifth Avenue. The impact of her fall was so severe that it crushed the car's roof, yet remarkably, Evelyn's body remained intact, seemingly composed in death.

The scene was quickly discovered by a passerby. Within minutes, Robert Wiles, a student at the nearby New York Institute of Photography, arrived at the scene. He took a photograph that would become one of the most famous images of the 20th century. The photograph captured Evelyn lying on the crumpled car roof, appearing almost serene, her legs crossed at the ankles, and her gloved left hand clutching a pearl necklace. The image was published in the May 12, 1947, edition of "Life" magazine, cementing its place in history.

Evelyn left a note for her sister-in-law in her purse, found on the observation deck. The note read:

"I don't want anyone in our family to see any part of me and you can dispose of my body by cremation and destroy the ashes. I beg of you and my family that they don't have any services for me or remembrances of me. My fiancé asked me to marry him in June. I don't think I would make a good wife for anyone. He is much better off without me."

From 1932 to 1947 a dozen people jumped from the observation deck. After five people tried to jump in a three-week span, a barrier was put in place to act as a deterrent. It served its purpose and there were no more incidents until 1970.

Perhaps the most gruesome suicide took place on August 26, 1981, when David Klugman, a 23-year-old Rockville Centre resident bought a ticket to the observation deck.

Once he got up there, he climbed a seven-foot-tall fence on the 86th floor. He lowered himself down to a ledge on the 85th floor, stripped naked and began meditating and praying as people rushed outside and yelled for him to stop. Klugman was unyielding as coldly inched closer to the end of the ledge and jumped to the unforgiving pavement on 34th Street below. According to firsthand accounts, blood splattered over one hundred feet onto people passing by.

After a handful of suicides in the early 21st century, the numbers of jumpers who have killed themselves currently stands at 36.

Not everyone who jumps off the Empire State Building has a death wish. Some seek the thrill, the rush of adrenaline, and the applause of those who witness their daring feats. Over the years, the iconic skyscraper has become a playground for daredevils looking to test their limits.

On April 24, 1986, two British daredevils, Michael McCarthy and Alisdair Boyd, embarked on a bold adventure. Both seasoned thrill-seekers from London, they arrived at the Empire State Building early in the morning, blending in with the crowd of tourists. With tickets in hand, they ascended to the observation deck, pretending to admire the breathtaking view of the New York City skyline.

As the clock struck 11 a.m., McCarthy and Boyd positioned themselves on an 18-inch-wide concrete retaining wall. They discreetly removed their coats and

sweaters, revealing parachute packs strapped to their backs. Without hesitation, the brazen daredevils scaled the 10-foot-high fence topped with curved steel spikes.

The onlookers gasped, and a nearby employee began shouting for them to stop, but the duo was already committed to their stunt.

With a synchronized leap, they plunged off the edge, the high winds catching their parachutes and carrying them two blocks away. Boyd, a master of his craft, expertly folded his parachute upon landing and quickly hailed a cab, disappearing into the city's labyrinthine streets. McCarthy, however, was not as fortunate. His parachute became entangled in a streetlamp on the corner of 31st Street and Fifth Avenue, leaving him dangling helplessly.

As the police arrived, McCarthy attempted to bluff his way out, claiming he was filming a scene for the next James Bond movie. His story quickly fell apart when he failed to produce a filming permit. McCarthy was arrested and charged with reckless endangerment, performing an exhibition without a permit, and unlawful parachuting.

A dozen years later, on October 24, 1998, two more daredevils decided to take the plunge. As dusk settled over the city around 6 p.m., the men, clad in blue jumpsuits, visited the observation deck. They strolled casually for a few minutes, seemingly just another pair of tourists soaking in the view.

Then, with a sudden burst of energy, they scaled the fence and leapt into the darkening sky. Pink parachutes blossomed behind them. The men floated gracefully to the ground, touching down safely on 34th Street. Though they disappeared into the night, one of the men was later identified as Thor Alex Kappfjell, a renowned Norwegian base jumper known for his audacious feats.

Shootings

Sadly, there have been two notable shootings at the Empire State Building. On February 23, 1997, the iconic skyscraper became the scene of a tragic event. Around 5:00 PM, a 69-year-old Palestinian teacher named Ali Hassan Abu Kamal entered the building. Kamal, who had come to the United States on a tourist visa, carried a .380-caliber Beretta handgun in his briefcase. After buying a ticket, he took the elevator to the observation deck on the 86th floor.

Without warning, Kamal pulled out his gun and began shooting. He fired at random, striking seven people. One of the victims, a Danish musician, was killed instantly. Six others were injured, some critically, as panic and chaos ensued among the visitors. The scene was one of terror as people scrambled to find safety, and emergency services rushed to the site.

After the brief but deadly spree, Kamal turned the gun on himself, firing a shot into his own head. He was critically injured and later died in the hospital. Investigations revealed that Kamal had been deeply troubled and despondent over personal and financial issues. In a note found in his hotel room, he expressed frustration and anger at the United States and Israel, but his exact motives remained a complex blend of personal despair and political discontent.

On August 24, 2012, the Empire State Building was once again the site of a deadly shooting. This time, the incident occurred just outside the building, at the intersection of 34th Street and Fifth Avenue. At around 9:00 AM, a disgruntled former clothing designer, Jeffrey Johnson, aged 58, shot and killed a former coworker.

Johnson had been laid off from his job at a women's accessories company, during the economic downturn. Holding a grudge against his coworker, whom he blamed for his dismissal, Johnson waited outside the office building where his target worked. As soon as his enemy arrived for the day, Johnson approached him, pulled out a .45-caliber semiautomatic handgun, and shot him in the head and torso, killing him instantly.

Witnesses to the shooting alerted nearby police officers who were stationed near the Empire State Building. As Johnson attempted to walk away from the scene, the officers confronted him. Johnson raised his weapon, prompting the officers to open fire. In the ensuing exchange, Johnson was killed, and nine bystanders were injured by stray bullets and ricochets.

Deadly Pennies

Among the myriad urban legends that swirl through New York City, one stands out for its blend of danger and intrigue: the tale of the deadly penny. According to this popular myth, a penny thrown from the top of the Empire State Building could kill someone on the street below if it struck them on the head. This legend, despite its persistence, is unequivocally false.

The Empire State Building, with its towering height and unique architecture, creates a complex aerodynamic environment. One key feature of this environment is the considerable updraft that occurs along the building's facade. This updraft means that objects, such as pennies, thrown from the observation deck often do not fall straight to the ground. Instead, they are frequently blown back against the structure, commonly landing on the window ledges of the 86th floor.

To debunk the myth of the deadly penny, it's essential to understand the concept of terminal velocity. Many people believe that an object, once dropped from a great height, will continue to accelerate until it hits the ground, potentially reaching lethal speeds. If this were true for a penny, it could theoretically reach speeds of around 193 miles per hour. However, in reality, the physics of falling objects tells another story.

As a penny falls, it is subjected to two primary forces: gravity, which pulls it downward, and air resistance, or drag, which pushes upward against it. Initially, gravity causes the penny to accelerate, increasing its velocity. But as the penny's speed increases, so does the air resistance it encounters. This upward force grows until it balances the downward pull of gravity.

The terminal velocity of an object is the constant speed it reaches when the forces of gravity and air resistance are equal and opposite. For a penny, this terminal velocity is around 65 miles per hour—significantly lower than the

193 miles per hour suggested by the myth. This difference is due to the drag force acting on the penny as it falls.

When a penny is dropped from a height, such as the top of the Empire State Building, it will accelerate until it has fallen approximately 43 meters. At this point, the force of gravity is perfectly counterbalanced by the force of air resistance, causing the penny to stop accelerating and continue falling at a constant speed — its terminal velocity.

Given the relatively low terminal velocity and the considerable updrafts around the Empire State Building, a penny thrown from the observation deck is highly unlikely to cause any harm. The next time someone tells you this story, please set the record straight: No one has ever been killed by a penny falling from the Empire State Building.

Hauntings

The Empire State Building, an architectural marvel and symbol of New York City's grandeur, has witnessed countless stories of ambition, triumph, and tragedy. With its storied history, it's no surprise that some believe the iconic skyscraper is haunted. Amidst the daily hustle and bustle, whispers of ghostly encounters echo through its halls, particularly centered around the 86th floor observation deck.

Over the years, multiple staff members and security personnel have reported seeing the apparition of a woman dressed in mid-20th century attire wandering the observation deck. This spectral figure, clad in period clothing, appears lost and forlorn, as if searching for something — or someone. Many believe this ghostly presence to be Evelyn McHale, a young woman who tragically jumped to her death from the 86th floor on May 1, 1947.

One current employee, who works on the observation deck, shared his experiences with me. He had never seen the ghostly woman that others had described, but he often felt her presence. "A few times a year, typically in the early morning hours when it's warm outside, I'll feel a woman's presence walking beside me," he confided. "It's not something you can see, but you feel it — a cold breeze, a shift in the air, like someone brushing past you."

His description matches the accounts of many other staff members who have sensed the same eerie presence. Some have reported hearing soft, muffled sobs, while others have felt an inexplicable chill even on warm days. The sensation of being watched or followed is common, especially during the quieter hours  when the observation deck is nearly empty.

Hotel Chelsea

Hotel Chelsea, an iconic landmark located on West 23rd Street, is steeped in history and cultural significance. Known for its distinctive red-brick façade, wrought-iron balconies, and Gothic Revival architecture, the Hotel Chelsea has been a beacon for artists, writers and musicians for over a century. Its halls have witnessed triumphs, tragedies, and tales that have become integral parts of New York City's rich cultural tapestry.

The story of Hotel Chelsea began in the late 19th century. Designed by the architect Philip Hubert, the building was completed in 1884 as one of the first private cooperative apartment buildings in New York City. Hubert's vision was to create a utopian community for the city's creative and intellectual elite, a place where artists and professionals could live and collaborate. The building's unique architecture, characterized by its Victorian Gothic elements, set it apart from other cookie-cutter residential buildings of the time.

Initially, the cooperative model flourished, attracting a diverse mix of residents. However, economic difficulties in the late 19th century led to the building's conversion into a hotel in 1905. The transformation marked the beginning of Hotel Chelsea's evolution into a cultural landmark.

Throughout the 20th century, Hotel Chelsea became synonymous with artistic innovation and bohemian lifestyle. Its affordable rates, spacious rooms, and welcoming atmosphere attracted a who's who of the creative world. The hotel's legacy was cemented by the notable figures who lived and worked within its walls.

The hotel has a long association with literary greats. Mark Twain, O. Henry, and Arthur C. Clarke are among the celebrated authors who stayed there. Clarke famously wrote "2001: A Space Odyssey" while living on site. The hotel also became a home to poets like Allen Ginsberg and Dylan Thomas. Thomas, a Welsh poet, famously spent his final days at the hotel drinking himself to death in 1953, allegedly after consuming 18 shots of whiskey at the nearby White Horse Tavern.

The hotel's allure extended to the music world as well. Bob Dylan, Janis Joplin, and Leonard Cohen were among the musicians who found inspiration at the Chelsea. Cohen's song "Chelsea Hotel #2" immortalized his brief romantic encounter with Janis Joplin at the hotel. The punk rock movement of the 1970s saw the hotel become a hub for musicians such as Patti Smith and Sid Vicious of the Sex Pistols.

The visual arts also thrived at Hotel Chelsea. Painters like Jackson Pollock and Robert Mapplethorpe, and filmmakers such as Stanley Kubrick, were drawn to the hotel's eclectic environment. The building's walls themselves became canvases, adorned with works by resident artists. Andy Warhol and his entourage were frequent visitors, and Warhol even filmed parts of his experimental films at the hotel. While researching for her role in the 1971 film, "Klute" actress Jane Fonda interviewed a number of local prostitutes. She would later win an Academy Award for her performance.

By the late 20th century, Hotel Chelsea faced financial difficulties and management challenges. The building's infrastructure deteriorated, and its once-vibrant creative community began to wane. In 2011, the hotel was sold to a developer, sparking concerns among residents and preservationists about its future. Renovations began, aiming to modernize the facilities while preserving the building's historic character.

The renovation process was fraught with delays and controversies, but by the mid-2010s, efforts to restore the hotel were in full swing. The goal was to retain the hotel's bohemian spirit while upgrading it to meet contemporary standards. Today, Hotel Chelsea is thriving as it offers a blend of historic charm and modern luxury.

Under Siege

In the gritty heart of New York City during the 1970s, Hotel Chelsea stood as a notorious haven for society's outcasts. Pimps, prostitutes, and other shadowy figures from the city's dark underbelly made it their home. The hotel's once-grand corridors echoed with the whispers of criminal activities, creating an atmosphere thick with danger.

As the city slept on the night of October 20, 1974, two men were gearing up for a sinister operation. Shortly after midnight, these gunmen stormed Hotel Chelsea, bringing with them a wave of terror. They moved with precision, their first act being the capture of two unsuspecting guests. The captives, bewildered and terrified, were herded into an elevator and taken to an empty room on the third floor. One gunman stood guard over them while the other prowled the hallways, seeking more victims.

The third floor was a hub of activity that night, with a party in full swing. Guests were gambling, playing poker, and momentarily oblivious to the danger lurking nearby. The second gunman infiltrated the party, his presence unnoticed until it was too late. Over the next six hours, the duo meticulously rounded up fifteen guests. Each person was stripped of their clothes, robbed of their cash and jewelry, and ruthlessly beaten. One lady was even raped. The victims were then crammed into a closet and bathroom, their hopes for escape dwindling with every passing minute.

By 6:30 am, the gunmen's spree had ended. They slipped out of the room, leaving their prisoners in shock. Desperate and frightened, the captives used the phone in the room to call the police. Within minutes, the hotel was swarming with officers. Twenty-five police officers scoured the building, but the gunmen had vanished, leaving behind no trace. As the bulk of the officers departed, four remained in the lobby, maintaining a presence at the crime scene.

At 9:30 am, an unexpected twist unfolded. The front desk received a call from a man on the first floor requesting his bill. A policeman, Officer Richard Abbinanti, overheard the conversation and became suspicious. The desk clerk, prompted by Abbinanti, inquired if the caller was alone or had company. Another hotel employee intervened, confirming that the man and his companion matched the descriptions of the gunmen.

Quick to act, Officer Abbinanti devised a plan. Disguised in a hotel bellhop uniform, he made his way to the suspects' room and knocked on the door. The man inside, wary and on edge, refused to open the door. Instead, he loudly asked about his bill, insisting he would slide the money under the door. Despite Abbinanti's persistent attempts to coax the man into opening up, he stood firm. After five tense minutes, Abbinanti kicked the door in as three other officers stormed the room. Chaos erupted.

One suspect lunged for a revolver but was quickly subdued. The other tried to escape through the window, only to be captured moments later. Police seized $1,881 in cash and a stash of stolen watches and rings. The men,

Aaron Legrando and Edward Steadley, both from Brooklyn, were arrested and charged with armed robbery, assault, rape, unlawful imprisonment, and possession of heroin.

Legrando and Steadley were sentenced to 25 years in prison.

Death Comes to the Hotel

For 140 years as tenants and guests have come and gone, one thing has remained constant at Hotel Chelsea- Death. The building has been the scene of numerous suicides, murders, and mysterious deaths, each adding a layer to its haunted legacy.

On January 27, 1908, Almyra Wilcox, a woman of means from Milwaukee, checked into Hotel Chelsea. She was a reclusive figure, seldom seen by other guests. Shortly after her arrival, she summoned a doctor who prescribed her morphine. With a heavy heart and a troubled mind, she consumed the entire bottle. Her lifeless body was discovered by a hotel staff member on February 2.

In October 1909, Frank Kavecky, treasurer of the Hungarian Benevolent Society, faced a dire predicament. While taking the subway in the Bronx, he was accosted by a robber wielding a knife. The thief demanded all his money, and Kavecky, who had just collected $1,200 in dues from society members, had no choice but to comply.

Terrified of being accused of stealing the funds, he fled to Manhattan and checked into Hotel Chelsea. In his room, he penned three letters: one to his wife, one to a friend, and one to the Hungarian Benevolent Society. In these letters, he explained his predicament, expressing his inability to bear the disgrace of being called a thief. With a heavy heart, he sat in a rocking chair, pulled out a revolver, and ended his life with a single shot to the head. Strangely, no one heard the gunshot. When a friend called the hotel looking for him, a bellboy climbed through the transom and discovered Kavecky's lifeless body in the chair.

On March 5, 1922, Etelka Graf, a 38-year-old Italian immigrant, was visiting her parents in Manhattan and staying on the fifth floor of Hotel Chelsea. Overcome by a sudden and severe bout of madness, she cut off her left hand with a pair of sewing scissors. In a state of shock and despair, she threw the severed hand under the bed and then jumped from her fifth-floor window. She landed on a third-floor balcony, suffering severe injuries. Both her ankles were broken, as well as her left arm, and she had deep cuts on her face and head. Despite being rushed to Bellevue Hospital, she was pronounced dead upon arrival, having succumbed to massive blood loss.

These stories, though separated by years, are bound by a common thread of tragedy and despair. However, the death the hotel is best known for took place on October 12, 1978.

John Simon Ritchie, known best as Sid Vicious, was a key figure in the punk rock movement of the 1970s. Known for his aggressive persona and self-destructive behavior, Vicious epitomized the rebellious spirit of punk rock.

Nancy Spungen, an American groupie and former go-go dancer known for her chaotic lifestyle, met Vicious in London in 1977. Their relationship was intense and volatile, fueled by heavy drug use and frequent conflicts.

In September 1978, after the Sex Pistols disbanded,  Vicious and Spungen moved into Room 100 of the Hotel Chelsea. The hotel, with its reputation as a haven for artists and musicians, seemed a fitting home for the troubled couple. However, their time there was marked by increasing instability and drug addiction.

On the night of October 11, 1978, Sid and Nancy were engaged in their usual routine of drug use, specifically heroin. Accounts suggest that both were heavily under the influence.

In the early hours of October 12, 1978, a disturbance was reported from Room 100. At around 11:00 a.m., Sid allegedly discovered Nancy lying under the bathroom sink, bleeding from a single stab wound to the abdomen. She was pronounced dead at the scene. The weapon, a 5-inch folding knife, was found nearby. It was later determined that the knife belonged to Sid Vicious.

A badly bruised Sid was immediately interrogated, arrested and charged with second-degree murder. He gave conflicting accounts of what happened that night, at one point claiming he had stabbed Nancy but did not mean to kill her, and at another point stating he did not remember anything from the night. His mother, Anne Beverley, later suggested that her son was too intoxicated to have committed the murder intentionally and posited that an unknown third party might have been involved.

While awaiting trial that would've put him behind bars for fifteen years, Sid Vicious was released on $50,000 bail posted by Virgin Records. However, his legal troubles were compounded by his continued drug use and a botched suicide attempt. On December 9, 1978, he was arrested again for assaulting Patti Smith's brother, Todd Smith, at a nightclub. Sid spent nearly two months in Rikers Island jail before being released on bail once more. On February 1, 1979, Sid Vicious attended a party celebrating his release. During the party, he overdosed on heroin and was found dead. He was 21 years old.

The death of Nancy Spungen and the subsequent demise of Sid Vicious have been the subject of much speculation and numerous investigations. Some theories suggest that Nancy's death was a botched robbery, or a drug deal gone wrong, but no definitive evidence has surfaced to support these claims. The incident remains a tragic and murky chapter in the history of the punk rock movement.

The room where the tragedy occurred, Room 100, has since been renovated and renumbered as 1F, but the memory of the events that transpired there lingers in the lore of the Chelsea Hotel.

Hauntings

When the Titanic sank in April 1912, many survivors were brought to New York City. Among the places that gave rooms to these traumatized individuals was Hotel Chelsea.

According to legend, a lady named Mary was the wife of a Titanic passenger who came to the hotel with hopes and dreams of reuniting with her beloved husband after he was rescued. Upon her arrival, she learned that her husband was among the many who had perished in the icy waters of the Atlantic. Overwhelmed by grief and despair, Mary found herself alone in a strange city, her dreams shattered.

Unable to cope with the devastating loss of her husband, Mary spiraled into deep depression. The pain of her husband's death was too much to bear. One fateful night, overcome by grief, Mary either hanged herself in her room or jumped from her balcony at Hotel Chelsea.

There is another version of Mary's story that some claim is the true account of her fate. According to this version, Mary was actually onboard the Titanic and survived the disaster. She arrived in New York with other survivors and checked into Hotel Chelsea. Despite surviving the sinking, the emotional scars left by the event, compounded by the loss of her husband, led her to take her own life in the hotel.

Mary's spirit is said to linger at Hotel Chelsea, eternally mourning the loss of her husband. Numerous guests and staff have reported eerie encounters and unexplained phenomena believed to be connected to her restless spirit. She is often seen as a spectral figure dressed in a flowing white gown, wandering the hallway on the fifth floor.

In 2024, I had the opportunity to stay at the legendary Hotel Chelsea. Known for its rich history and reputation for being haunted, I couldn't resist the allure of experiencing its eerie charm firsthand. Upon checking in, I requested a haunted room, hoping to catch a glimpse of the supernatural. The concierge, with a knowing smile, assigned me a room on the first floor.

Most of my stay at Hotel Chelsea was uneventful. I explored Manhattan and spent my evenings working on my computer.

It was around 10 p.m. when a strange event occurred. I was sitting at the table, working on this book. The room was quiet. Suddenly, I heard a faint rattling sound. I turned around and saw a coffee mug resting on a saucer on the cabinet behind me. The mug was shaking slightly, creating a soft clinking noise as it vibrated against the saucer.

I stared at the mug in disbelief, my mind racing to find a rational explanation. Was it the subway causing the vibrations? But then I remembered I was on the first floor, not the ground floor, and the vibrations from the subway wouldn't reach this level. As soon as I got up to inspect the mug, it stopped shaking abruptly. I stood there for a moment, unsure of what had happened.

For the rest of my stay, the room remained eerily silent. The mug never rattled again, and no other strange events occurred.

When it was time to check out, I decided to mention the incident to the front desk clerk. A gentleman with a friendly demeanor was handling my checkout. Casually, I recounted the story of the shaking mug and my initial thoughts about the subway vibrations. He listened attentively, then checked the computer for my room number.

As soon as he saw where I had been staying, he chuckled. "Well, you were on the first floor! It happens," he said with a smile. His casual response left me both intrigued and amused. It seemed that my experience was not unique, but rather a common occurrence for those staying at the hotel.

Photographs From Beyond

Spirit Photography

Spiritualism, which began in the 1840s, gained significant momentum during and after the Civil War. After an unprecedented loss of life, with an estimated 620,000 to 750,000 soldiers dead, and countless more injured or missing, the widespread loss prompted a surge in public interest in the afterlife and spiritual communication. People were eager for any form of proof that their loved ones continued to exist in some form, and spiritualism offered that hope.

During that time spirit photography, a practice claiming to capture images of spirits or ghosts, emerged and became a popular phenomenon during the height of the spiritualist movement.

The practice of spirit photography began in the early 1860s with William H. Mumler, an engraver and amateur photographer in Boston. Mumler claimed he accidentally captured the image of a deceased relative while taking a self-portrait. This accidental discovery spurred interest in the possibility of photographing spirits, and Mumler quickly began offering his services to the public.

Word quickly spread of Mumler's ability to capture ghostly apparitions hovering beside or behind his grief-stricken clients. One notable customer was Mary Todd Lincoln, who wanted to connect with her deceased husband, President Abraham Lincoln. Mumler's work became highly popular among spiritualists and those mourning lost loved ones. After a while the people of Boston became skeptical of Mumler's work and he moved his operation to New York where he opened a gallery on Broadway in a building owned by William Silver, another photographer. Mumler worked out a deal to buy out Silver and keep him around to help out. Mumler thrived in the Big Apple and made a fortune off of grieving New Yorkers. For one photo with a deceased loved one, Mumler charged $5 to $10, which is equivalent to $200 to $400 in 2024.

With so much money to be made, there were some tricks to Mumler's trade. The practice of spirit photography was rife with chicanery, involving various photographic tricks and deceptive techniques to create the illusion of ghostly apparitions.

Photographers would expose the same photographic plate twice, first capturing the image of the living subject and then overlaying it with a second image of a person dressed in ghostly attire or an existing photograph of a deceased person. This created a superimposed effect, making it appear as though a spirit was present in the final photograph.

Another trick was composite printing. This technique involved combining two separate negatives, one of the living subject and one of the supposed spirit, to produce a single print. Composite printing allowed for greater control over the placement and appearance of the ghostly figure.

Some spirit photographers manually altered negatives or prints, adding ghostly images or effects using paint or scratching techniques. This method was used to create more subtle and mysterious apparitions.

In February 1869, P. V. Hickey went to the Silver and Mumler gallery and sat for a photograph. When he came back the next day to pick up his picture, he was presented with a photograph of himself along with a faded shadowy outline of a man standing next to him. Hickey became suspicious and went straight to the mayor's office and filed a complaint. Joseph Tooker, a marshal, went to investigate and paid for a sitting. When he got his photograph, a spirit was also seen in the picture. Hickey went back a second time and got another photo taken. Strangely, when he looked at it, the image of Marshal Tooker was standing beside him.

A complaint with the New York District Attorney was filed and William Mumler and William Silver were both arrested and charged with fraud. Silver was released but

Mumler was accused of duping people with his phony spirit pictures.

The trial was held at the Tombs Court House, attracting widespread public and media attention. It was a case that not only questioned Mumler's integrity but also the validity of spiritualism itself.

William H. Mumler's trial was a sensational affair, drawing crowds of spectators and a cadre of prominent lawyers and experts. The prosecution, led by Elbridge T. Gerry, sought to prove that Mumler's photographs were fraudulent, created through trickery rather than genuine spiritual phenomena. The prosecution's case hinged on the testimony of expert photographers and witnesses who had investigated Mumler's methods.

One of the key witnesses for the prosecution was P.T. Barnum, the famous showman and skeptic. Barnum was a well-known critic of spiritualism and had a history of exposing mediums and spiritualist practices that he believed were fraudulent. His skepticism was rooted in his extensive experience with show business and his understanding of how easily people could be deceived by illusions and trickery.

To prove his point about Mumler's spirit photographs, Barnum decided to commission a photograph from Abraham Bogardus that featured him with the ghost of Abraham Lincoln to demonstrate how easily existing photographs could be manipulated to create the illusion of a spirit presence.

The defense, led by John D. Townsend, argued that
Mumler's work was genuine and that he was being
unfairly persecuted for his unconventional beliefs.
Townsend called upon satisfied customers who testified
to the authenticity of the spirit photographs and the
comfort they had provided. Among these witnesses was

Luther Colby, editor of the spiritualist newspaper "Banner of Light," who passionately defended Mumler's character and work. William Silver, Mumler's partner, also was grilled on the stand. He maintained that he was not a spiritualist, but he could not explain how Mumler had created the images because he had never seen Mumler do anything nefarious in their gallery.

After weeks of testimony and heated arguments, the trial concluded. Since the prosecution couldn't prove with 100% certainty that Mumler had faked his images, he was acquitted. The verdict was met with mixed reactions. Spiritualists celebrated the outcome as a vindication of their beliefs, while skeptics viewed it as a failure of the justice system to protect the public from fraud.

Despite his acquittal, Mumler's career never fully recovered from the trial. The intense scrutiny and ongoing skepticism surrounding his work led to a decline in his business. He continued to practice photography but never regained the same level of prominence he once enjoyed.

From Author to Spiritualist

Sir Arthur Conan Doyle was born on May 22, 1859, in Edinburgh, Scotland. His father, Charles Altamont Doyle, was an artist and civil servant, while his mother, Mary Foley Doyle, was a well-educated and imaginative woman who greatly influenced young Arthur's storytelling abilities. Despite his family's financial struggles, Arthur received an excellent education, attending Jesuit preparatory school Stonyhurst College, followed by a year at a Jesuit school in Austria.

In 1876, Doyle began his medical studies at the University of Edinburgh, where he met several notable figures, including Dr. Joseph Bell, a professor whose keen observation skills and logical reasoning later inspired the character of Sherlock Holmes. Doyle graduated in 1881 and embarked on a varied medical career, working as a ship's doctor on a whaling vessel and later on a voyage to West Africa. These experiences not only broadened his horizons but also provided material for his future writings.

Practicing medicine in Southsea, Hampshire, Doyle began to seriously pursue writing. His first significant work, "A Study in Scarlet," introduced the world to Sherlock Holmes and his loyal friend, Dr. John Watson. Published in 1887, the novel received modest success, but it wasn't until the serialized stories in "The Strand Magazine" that Holmes became a literary sensation. Stories such as "The Adventures of Sherlock Holmes" and "The Memoirs of Sherlock Holmes" captivated readers, establishing Doyle as a master of the detective genre.

Despite his success with Sherlock Holmes, Doyle grew weary of his creation and killed off the detective in "The Final Problem" hoping to focus on more serious literary works. However, public demand eventually led him to resurrect Holmes in "The Hound of the Baskervilles", set before Holmes' supposed death, and later fully in "The Adventure of the Empty House".

Beyond his detective fiction, Doyle was a prolific writer, producing historical novels and science fiction works along with various short stories, plays, and non-fiction pieces.

Although he was successful, in his personal life, Doyle experienced much sadness. He married Louisa Hawkins in 1885, with whom he had two children, Mary and Kingsley. After Louisa's death from tuberculosis in 1906, Doyle immersed himself in spiritualism, which was a belief in the ability to communicate with the spirits of the dead. It became a significant part of his life, shaping his later years and works.

Doyle's fascination with the supernatural grew after the death of his son, Kingsley, in 1918 from pneumonia following injuries sustained during World War I. This profound loss, coupled with the deaths of other close family members, including his brother, two brothers-in-law, and two nephews, deepened his quest for answers beyond the physical world.

In his pursuit of spiritual understanding, Doyle became a prominent figure in the spiritualist movement. Doyle's first significant contact with the spiritualist community was through Pennsylvania medium Ethel Post-Parrish, who claimed to channel spirits. He was reportedly moved by her ability to provide detailed and personal messages from the deceased. This experience reinforced his belief in the afterlife and convinced him of the legitimacy of spiritualist practices.

Doyle's involvement in séances extended beyond personal loss; he actively sought to investigate and validate the phenomenon. He traveled extensively to attend séances and meet with renowned mediums of the time, including Eusapia Palladino, Mina "Margery" Crandon, and William Hope. Doyle documented these experiences in his writings, providing detailed accounts of the séances and the messages he received.

One of Doyle's most notable séances involved a Boston medium named Mina Crandon, known as "Margery." Crandon was reputed to have extraordinary abilities, including materializing spirits and producing physical phenomena. Doyle attended several séances with her and was convinced of her authenticity. Despite skepticism and accusations of fraud from others, Doyle defended Crandon, believing that her abilities provided undeniable proof of the spirit world.

Doyle also conducted séances at his own home in Surrey, England, inviting friends and family to participate. These gatherings were often led by his second wife, Jean Leckie, who shared his spiritualist beliefs and claimed to have mediumistic abilities. Jean often served as the medium, attempting to contact their deceased loved ones, including Kingsley and Doyle's first wife, Louisa. Doyle believed that these personal séances brought him closer to his lost family members and provided comfort in his grief. In his writings, Doyle detailed his belief in life after death and his conviction that communication with the spirit world was not only possible but also beneficial for the living. According to him, Spiritualism "absolutely removes all fear of death. Secondly it bridges death for those dear ones we may lose."

Doyle's involvement with spirit photography was a particularly intriguing aspect of his beliefs. Spirit photography fascinated Doyle. He became a staunch defender of some practitioners of this art, believing that their work provided tangible evidence of the afterlife. (Even though the image was created by some chicanery.)

One of the spirit photography cases that Doyle supported was that of the Cottingley Fairies. In 1920, two young cousins, Elsie Wright and Frances Griffiths, claimed to have photographed fairies near their home in Cottingley, England. The photographs showed the girls interacting with small, ethereal beings. Doyle, eager for proof of the supernatural, endorsed the photographs in an article for "The Strand Magazine," and later in his book "The Coming of the Fairies". He believed the photos were authentic, despite skepticism from many.

Doyle's advocacy for spirit photography and other aspects of spiritualism often brought him into conflict with skeptics, most notably the famous magician and escape artist Harry Houdini. Houdini, once a friend of Doyle, was a fervent debunker of spiritualist frauds. Their differing views on spiritualism led to a public and personal rift. Doyle believed that Houdini possessed supernatural powers but refused to acknowledge them, while Houdini was committed to exposing fraudulent mediums and spiritualist practices.

Despite the controversies and criticisms, Doyle remained unwavering in his beliefs. He continued to lecture on spiritualism and travel to investigate phenomena.

On May 5, 1922, Sir Arthur Conan Doyle filled Carnegie Hall in New York City with an audience eager to hear his views on the spirit world. The evening covered a range of topics, from ectoplasm to rescue circles, and showcased Doyle's unwavering conviction in the afterlife.

Doyle began his lecture by discussing "rescue circles," which he described as places where earthbound spirits could be found. These circles, according to Doyle, were prevalent in England, serving as havens for spirits unable to move on to the next realm. He recounted a personal experience involving one such spirit, which had caused significant distress for a family in England.

The family, sharing their house with the mischievous spirit, had been tormented by incessant noise in the attic at night, depriving them of sleep. Doyle, known for his investigative spirit, visited the house to communicate with the ghost. The spirit revealed that it was searching for important papers it believed were hidden in the attic. Doyle promised to help and conducted a thorough search but found nothing. He then convinced the spirit that the papers were not there, leading to its departure and restoring peace to the household.

Transitioning from rescue circles, Doyle delved into the mechanics of spirit photography, a topic that fascinated him deeply. He drew an analogy between transmitting telegraphs and capturing images on photographic plates. Just as telegraphs transmitted messages over distances, Doyle explained, the process of capturing spirits in photographs involved a similar transmission of energy.

Doyle passionately argued that spirits desired to be photographed, wanting to be seen by their loved ones left behind. He presented this as evidence that the spirit world sought connection with the living, using photography as a medium.

To support his claims, Doyle shared several spirit photographs, beginning with three taken in New York by Miss Sanders, a member of the Psychical Research Society. These images, according to Doyle, provided clear evidence of spirits captured alongside the living. The photographs showed ethereal figures, their presence unmistakable and haunting.

Doyle then presented a photograph taken by William Hope, a renowned spirit photographer from Crewe, England. The image depicted a nine-year-old boy standing beside his father, a spectral figure appearing beside the living man.

Doyle used this photograph to illustrate his point that spirits, especially those of loved ones, sought to be seen and remembered.

Throughout the lecture, Doyle's passion and conviction were palpable. He spoke as a man who had experienced profound loss and found hope in the belief of an afterlife. His dedication to spiritualism, despite widespread skepticism, showcased his relentless pursuit of knowledge beyond the material world.

Doyle photographed with the spirit of his first wife

Although controversial, Doyle's views did not diminish his literary reputation; rather, they added a complex dimension to his legacy. Doyle's commitment to spiritualism and his willingness to champion what he believed to be the truth, even in the face of widespread skepticism, showcased his enduring quest for knowledge and his deep compassion for those seeking comfort from overwhelming grief.

Gotham Gore

The Lower Manhattan Slasher

In May 1981, the slasher film "Friday the 13th Part 2" dominated the box office, cementing Jason Voorhees as a horror icon with a massive following. Little did New York City know that a month later, the Big Apple would face a real-life horror story that would leave its residents gripped with fear. This terrifying saga began on the night of June 27, 1981, when a man who would become known as the Lower Manhattan Slasher embarked on a brutal spree that would haunt the city's streets.

It was a warm summer night in Sara D. Roosevelt Park when 41-year-old Charles Edwards lay asleep on a bench. His slumber was violently interrupted by a searing pain on the right side of his neck. Groggy and disoriented, Edwards realized he was bleeding profusely. As he screamed for help, a police officer patrolling the park rushed to his aid and quickly transported him to New York-Presbyterian Lower Manhattan Hospital. Edwards had been slashed, and the city was about to discover that he was just the first victim.

Around 11:30 p.m. that same night, Miguel Ancarmacion, a 30-year-old drifter, stumbled into St. Vincent's Hospital, drenched in blood. In a state of shock, Ancarmacion recounted his harrowing experience to the hospital staff. He had been sleeping on a bench in Washington Square Park when he awoke to a terrifying sight: blood pouring from his neck and a shadowy figure fleeing the scene. The police quickly realized that these two attacks were connected, signaling the emergence of a serial slasher.

As the night wore on, the police received more distressing reports. In Madison Square Park, three men—Gus Loges, Willie Townsend, and Lawrence Ruchman—were attacked while sleeping. Each man suffered cuts to the neck, and all three were rushed to St. Vincent's Hospital for treatment. Despite their injuries, they were able to provide descriptions of their assailant. According to the victims, the attacker was a stocky African American man, approximately 5'9" tall, wearing a maroon jacket, carpenter pants, and black slippers. His scruffy, unshaven appearance suggested he had been living on the streets for several days.

The police now had a clear picture of the slasher, but before they could mobilize and blanket the area, more attacks occurred. Charles Vann and Jerome Jordim were ambushed on Eighth Avenue, each suffering slashes to their necks. A short time later, Robert Brown was attacked while walking to a taxi station near Penn Station. All three men were taken to Bellevue Hospital, their wounds adding to the growing tally of victims.

New York City was gripped with fear. The attacks were seemingly random, and the slasher's ability to strike in different locations within a short period of time made him elusive and unpredictable. The media dubbed the assailant the Lower Manhattan Slasher, and the police were under immense pressure to capture him before more lives were lost.

In the days that followed, the NYPD increased patrols and urged the public to remain vigilant. Flyers with the slasher's description were distributed throughout the city, and detectives worked around the clock to piece together clues and identify potential suspects. Despite their efforts, the slasher remained at large, his identity and motive shrouded in mystery.

The NYPD was in a state of frantic urgency following the initial spree of the Lower Manhattan Slasher. With eight victims all miraculously surviving their encounters, the slasher's precise targeting of the neck left investigators baffled. The attacks were methodical, deep enough to cause significant bleeding but not fatal. A psychologist was brought in to develop a profile of the attacker, suggesting a deeply disturbed individual with a complex relationship to violence. The police, in response, increased patrols in parks and other areas where homeless individuals were known to sleep, hoping to prevent further attacks.

Despite heightened vigilance, the slasher struck again on June 30. The seventh victim, Roy Miley, was attacked while sleeping on a bench in Stuyvesant Park. The pattern was unmistakable, yet the increased patrols and public awareness seemed to push the slasher deeper into the shadows.

The slasher re-emerged with terrifying intensity on the night of July 5. At around 11 p.m., Roy Miller, a 25-year-old Brooklyn native, was standing on the corner of Chrystie and Delancey Streets when the slasher struck. Miller, bleeding profusely from his neck, was rushed to Bellevue Hospital. There, he provided a critical clue: his attacker resembled the sketch of the slasher but was clean-shaven.

While Miller was being treated, the slasher continued his rampage. An unknown vagrant in Sara D. Roosevelt Park became the next victim, suffering a particularly gruesome cut described by the first officer on the scene: "You could put your fist in there, the cut was so deep." The slasher was now escalating his violence.

Within hours, Richard Garfola was attacked on the steps of a building on Lafayette Street, sustaining a nine-inch gash across his neck. Shortly after, Harold Wilson was slashed and later died at Bellevue Hospital. The night culminated with two more victims, William Hurburt and Robert Packingham, both attacked in quick succession.

With 15 victims now claimed by the slasher, the NYPD was on full alert. At 2:45 a.m. on July 6, officers spotted a suspicious man on the corner of Prince and Wooster Streets in SoHo, matching the slasher's description. Notably, the man had blood on the pocket of his pants. When approached by the police, he became violent and attempted to flee. After a brief struggle, backup was called, and the suspect was subdued. A jagged, broken straight razor stained with blood was found in his bloody pocket.

The suspect, identified as 35-year-old Charles Sears, was immediately taken into custody. Sears' attorney initially planned an insanity defense, but after negotiations, Sears pleaded guilty to one charge of attempted murder for the attack on Roy Miley. However, he later withdrew his plea, claiming his lawyer was "subject to voodoo practiced by my family".

In February 1984, Sears was declared unfit to stand trial and was sent to the Mid-Hudson Psychiatric Center for treatment. After being deemed fit to stand trial later, he was transferred to Rikers Island to await his day in court

At Rikers Island, Sears managed to blend into the general population quietly. However, on August 1, 1985, an argument over a payphone with fellow inmate John Velez turned violent. Velez, incarcerated for robbery, used a makeshift knife to stab Sears multiple times in the chest, elbow, and knee. Sears managed to stagger back to his cell, where a guard discovered him. He was rushed to Elmhurst Hospital Center but succumbed to his injuries due to severe blood loss.

The Lower Manhattan Slasher's violent end at Rikers Island closed the chapter on one of the most harrowing episodes in the city's history.

Cropsey

Every town has their own version of a boogeyman.
Parents tell stories all over the world to dissuade their
mischievous children from venturing too far from home
or staying out past dusk. Tales of an evil Hookman in
Pennsylvania or the malevolent Bell Witch in Tennessee
have been passed on in their respective regions.

The legend of Cropsey, a menacing figure said to haunt
the woodlands of
Staten Island, has
been a chilling
staple of New
York urban
folklore for
decades. Over
time, this
phantom would
evolve, taking on
a more horrifying
reality in the
form of a real-life
convicted
kidnapper whose
crimes in the
1970s and 1980s
cast a dark
shadow over the
Big Apple.

The origins of the Cropsey legend are not entirely clear, but the story began to take shape in the 1960s and 1970s. Cropsey was said to be an escaped mental patient, a former asylum orderly who snapped, or a disfigured hermit who resided in the abandoned ruins of the old tuberculosis wards and the Willowbrook State School.

The connection between the Cropsey legend and Willowbrook is particularly significant. Willowbrook was a state-supported institution for children with intellectual disabilities, infamous for its deplorable conditions. Exposed by Geraldo Rivera in a 1972 exposé, the institution embodied the worst fears of neglect and abuse in a supposed care facility, making it a fertile ground for horrifying tales. The school was eventually closed in 1987 following public outcry and legal challenges.

As the years passed, Cropsey evolved from a nebulous

figure of admonition into a more defined character in urban lore. Descriptions of Cropsey varied—some said he wielded an axe, others claimed he had a hook for a hand, reflecting the typical embellishments of urban legends. Cropsey was said to lurk in the forests and abandoned buildings of Staten Island, hunting for children who dared to explore these forbidden areas. Over the years the legend became intertwined with a local vagrant named Andre Rand.

Andre Rand was born Frank Rushan on March 11, 1944. But after a few scrapes with the law, he changed his name. Using the alias of Frank Bruchette, Rand began working at various odd jobs around Staten Island. Rand was also employed by Willowbrook and worked there as a custodian, orderly and physical therapy aide, which is where he likely developed his predatory habits.

For many years Rand lived in makeshift camps in the dense woods of Staten Island near the institution. He is believed to have killed at least six people from 1972 to 1981.

The link between Rand and Cropsey solidified with the disappearance of a 12-year-old girl with Down syndrome who vanished in 1987. The girl was last seen with the balding, toothless 43-year-old vagrant, and after a frantic 35-day search conducted by 300 police officers, 100 volunteers, seven hound dogs and a psychic, her body was found buried in a shallow grave near Rand's campsite on the grounds of the abandoned Willowbrook facility. This discovery led to Rand's arrest and eventual conviction for kidnapping. He was later charged with the kidnapping of other children who had disappeared in the area over the years, though not all the bodies were found.

At 80 years old, Andre Rand is currently serving two consecutive twenty-five year to life prison sentences. Behind bars, he has allegedly confessed to other inmates about murdering at least one of his supposed victims.

The Cropsey legend and Andre Rand's crimes had a profound impact on Staten Island as well as the other four boroughs. For the residents of Staten Island, the boundaries between the imagined dangers of the Cropsey legend and the real-world horror represented by Rand were forever blurred. The fear was not only of a mythical boogeyman but of the very real possibility that someone living among them could perpetrate such horrors.

The Long Island Sea Monster

A Sea Serpent of Grand Proportions

In the summer of 1894, whispers began to circulate along the coasts of New Jersey, New York, and into the Long Island Sound — a mysterious creature, a sea serpent of grand proportions, had been sighted by fishermen and steamboat captains alike. Accounts varied, some claiming the creature stretched a mere 20 feet, while others insisted

it exceeded an astonishing 100 feet in length.

On July 16, 1895, Captain William Hazard and his crew were navigating the waters en route to New Haven, Connecticut. Suddenly, their routine journey took a startling turn when they encountered a massive brown object, roughly sixty feet in length, thrashing about in the water. The crew's initial shock turned to awe as the creature came into view under the beam of their searchlight, revealing scales that shimmered like jewels and eyes that glowed with an otherworldly intensity. This encounter not only provided visual confirmation of the creature's existence but also sparked widespread speculation and fascination among sailors and townsfolk alike.

Later that same night, Captain John Lisle, a seasoned seafarer native to Long Island, found himself face-to-face with the sea serpent as it glided through the harbor waters. In a moment of surreal clarity, the creature raised its massive head six feet above the water's surface, dwarfing Lisle's whaleboat in comparison. His vivid description of the creature as long as his boat and as large as a barrel lent credence to the reports circulating among locals. Lisle's firsthand account added a tangible sense of urgency and apprehension to the growing narrative surrounding the mysterious sea serpent.

A few days later, Theo Railey, an English vacationer seeking respite from the summer heat in Bay Ridge, found himself in a harrowing encounter with the elusive creature. Hoping to escape the stifling air of his lodgings, Theo decided to embark on a daring nighttime swim in the cool waters of the Atlantic Ocean. Armed with nothing more than a raft and the light of the full moon, Theo ventured into the dark waters, unaware of the terror that awaited him beneath the surface.

As Theo paddled further from the safety of the shore, he began to notice peculiar disturbances in the water around him — odd little bubbles rising to the surface, hinting at unseen movements lurking below. Undeterred, Theo pressed on, the gentle lapping of the waves serving as his only companion in the darkness.

Suddenly, Theo's trip took a terrifying turn when he felt a disturbance in the water beside him. With a jolt of fear, he realized that something massive and unseen was lurking beneath the surface. As Theo watched in horror, a large, mysterious creature began to circle his raft.

As the creature drew closer, Theo's senses were overwhelmed by its sheer size and ferocity. He described it as several hundred feet long, with four rows of teeth in each jaw and a half-dozen eyes.

Frozen in fear, Theo remained motionless as the creature circled his raft, its massive head rising "as big as the dome of St. Paul's" to peer down at him with an inscrutable gaze.

In that moment, time seemed to stand still as Theo grappled with the realization that he was utterly at the mercy of this ancient and mysterious monster.

Suddenly, without warning, the creature lunged, seizing Theo's right foot in its powerful jaws and pulling him into a desperate struggle for survival. Enraged and terrified, Theo fought back with all his strength, delivering blows to the creature's massive form in a desperate bid to free himself from its grasp. The ensuing struggle was a blur of fear and adrenaline, as Theo grappled with the creature in a battle for his very life.

In a moment of desperation, Theo managed to break free from the creature's grip, sending it fleeing into the dark waters of the Atlantic. As the creature vanished from sight, leaving only ripples in its wake, Theo's relief was tempered by the realization that he had narrowly escaped a fate worse than death. Gathering his wits, Theo made his way back to shore, his mind reeling with the horrors of his encounter. It was only upon reaching the safety of land that he discovered a grisly reminder of his ordeal— two teeth from the creature's powerful jaws lodged in his shoe.

The sightings continued, with the creature's presence confirmed in Hempstead Harbor and Matinecock Point, sparking widespread fascination and fear. Reports flooded the local papers, drawing curious onlookers and instilling a cautious reluctance to venture into the waters.

July 24th brought a significant development— an encounter with the creature in Hempstead Harbor prompted further speculation and scrutiny. Witnesses aboard a sailboat observed the serpent's approach,

prompting a hasty retreat as it dove beneath their vessel, leaving a trail of baffled observers in its wake.

As the summer wore on, sightings persisted, with accounts emerging from Oyster Bay, City Island, and beyond. The creature's mysterious presence cast a shadow over the region, its immense form stirring a mixture of awe and trepidation among those who dared to venture near the water's edge.

July 27th brought confirmation from unexpected sources—three United States Army officers reported a sighting of the creature in the Long Island Sound, adding weight to the growing body of evidence.

Three days later, staff at Blackwell's Island Hospital were astounded to discover a peculiar sight—a large log floating offshore near the island. Initially mistaken for a mere piece of driftwood, closer inspection revealed something altogether more astonishing. What had at first appeared to be a log was, in fact, a massive serpent, its lifeless form bobbing gently in the waters of the Long Island Sound.

With a mixture of trepidation and curiosity, hospital staff wasted no time in rowing out to investigate the strange apparition. As they drew closer, it became apparent that the creature was indeed deceased, its massive frame suggesting a creature of considerable size and strength.

Upon closer inspection, it became clear that the creature had suffered significant trauma, with signs of injury visible along its body. They also found several peculiarities about the creature's appearance. Its body, measuring an impressive 25 feet in length with a circumference of nine inches, was covered in scales. Strangely, there were no gills present, suggesting that the creature may have possessed unique adaptations for surviving beneath the waves.

Most peculiar of all was the discovery of a rope around the creature's neck, hinting at the possibility that it had been captured or even kept as a pet before meeting its untimely death. Equally perplexing was the large section of skin missing from its body. The creature had sustained severe burns along its body—a discovery that only deepened the mystery. Speculation ran rampant among the hospital staff as to the cause of these injuries.

However, further investigation uncovered a startling revelation: the burns were not the result of some fiery encounter in the depths of the ocean, but rather a tragic accident that occurred aboard a passing steamship. It was learned that the serpent had inadvertently coiled itself around a stove on the ship's forward deck, its massive form coming into contact with the scorching heat of the metal.

The intense heat had seared the creature's scales and flesh, inflicting grievous wounds upon its massive form.

Was the large snake found on Blackwell's Island the sea serpent? The boa's demise did little to quell public fascination, as people claimed to still see a large sea serpent in the Long Island Sound. Rumors swirled, with theories ranging from escaped pets to mythical monsters.

August 15th brought a startling development—a steamboat passing through Eaton's Neck collided with a massive sea creature, its size and appearance aligning with previous descriptions of the elusive sea serpent.

Eyewitness accounts described a creature nearly 100 feet in length. The damage wrought by the collision, including a broken paddle wheel and widespread panic among the crew, underscored the danger posed by the mysterious creature lurking beneath the waves.

By the end of the summer, sightings became rarer in New York. However, in New Jersey, people began to report seeing a large creature in the ocean. Willard Shaw, a wealthy lawyer whose summer cottage was in Spring Lake, New Jersey, was the first to come forward.

One balmy evening, as Shaw and his family relaxed on the porch, a commotion stirred the tranquil atmosphere. Mrs. Shaw was the first to spot the disturbance — a large, serpent thrashing in the nearby waters. With a sense of mounting curiosity, Shaw's son fetched a pair of binoculars, his excitement palpable as he trained them on the mysterious spectacle unfolding before them.
"It's a big snake!" the young boy exclaimed, his voice

trembling with awe and wonder. Both adults leaned in to peer through the binoculars, their eyes widening in astonishment at the sight before them. What they beheld defied all logic and reason — a colossal sea serpent, thrashing in the water.

Willard Shaw speculated that the creature measured anywhere from 75 to 100 feet in length, its head bearing a striking resemblance to that of an alligator — an eerie fusion of reptilian features and aquatic prowess.
In the days that followed, word of Shaw's sighting spread like wildfire, further fueling the fervor surrounding the sea monster.

Several months later, Captain Charles, a seasoned seaman with decades of experience navigating the vast waters of the Atlantic saw the creature. On this particular day, he found himself aboard a steamboat, leading a filibustering expedition into the waters not far from the shores of Atlantic City, New Jersey.

As the crew was settling in for a day at sea, the tranquility of the moment was suddenly shattered by a burst of excitement. As all eyes turned to the source of the commotion, a sight beyond belief greeted the crew — a colossal sea serpent, jet-black and sinuous, gracefully gliding through the waves. The creature's presence, stretching an estimated 75 to 100 feet in length, inspired a mixture of awe and disbelief among the crew.

Peterson and his crew watched in astonishment as the sea serpent's horse-like head emerged from the water, its sleek form cutting through the waves with an air of graceful majesty. The creature's smooth, ebony skin glistened in the sunlight, its powerful movements evoking a sense of ancient power and mystery. Peterson's description of the sea serpent as resembling an enormous smooth-skinned serpent with an alligator-like head.

As the sea serpent continued its journey, its path gradually carried it away from the coast, disappearing into the boundless horizon of the open sea. Peterson and his crew watched in awe as the creature's jet-black form receded into the distance. It was the last reported sighting.

Though the saga of the Long Island Sound Sea Serpent may have faded from public consciousness in the years that followed, its legacy endures—a testament to the enduring allure of the unknown and the timeless mysteries of the deep.

Printed in the USA
CPSIA information can be obtained
at www.ICGtesting.com
LVHW010432230824
789004LV00009B/186